CJ's Old Fashioned
Cook Book

CJ's Old Fashioned
Cook Book

Carolyn Jean Franklin Allen

Order this book online at www.trafford.com
or email orders@trafford.com

Most Trafford titles are also available at major online book retailers.

Printed in the United States of America.

ISBN: 978-1-4269-6892-1 (sc)
ISBN: 978-1-4269-6893-8 (e)

Trafford rev. 05/05/2011

www.trafford.com

North America & International
toll-free: 1 888 232 4444 (USA & Canada)
phone: 250 383 6864 ♦ fax: 812 355 4082

Introduction

    I grew up in country parts of Shreveport, LA where Working was number one on a daily basis. My grandmother, better known to all as lilmama, was the most marvelous homemade cook I have ever known. I love being In the kitchen watching her make up homemade recipes and use different ingredients to make a soulful dish. Lilmama made the family favorites. Especially on holidays, And on Sunday, she would be in the kitchen around 5 a.m. To start cooking for the day, She prepared the Sunday breakfast and dinner. But memories of her great skill as a cook is always an inspiration a brief portrait, my most treasured recipes, and my family's recipes are included in this book. The family is the strong tie that holds me to the ground, when it seems that I have lost, all that I had found. Lilmama always said "I love you for the top of your head to the bottom of your little toe," "take care with love and give love", to assure us of her undying love. My family are the rocks that hold me down, when I start to float away, and they can turn my life around, when I go astray. When lilmama wants to bring smiles to the faces around the dinning table, she features pies and cakes for dessert. Nothing seem to make a mealtime occasion quite so special as do these sweet favorites with their crisp crusts and varied fillings. From my kitchen to your, I welcome great food. I try to add a special touch to my dinner. You'll be so glad that I did. There's one for every occasion. Some Meals prepare, some help me balance my budget and other are simply good eating. Some lets me out of the kitchen while it bakes. When life treats me rough, my broken heart they will mend. Although sometimes I may fuss and fight And may not always agree. In the dark, they are the light. That shows the path so I can see. The most valuable suggestion [can offer you is to trust my recipes. I cook with my soul and most importantly with my heart and treasured recipes and food memories on these pages. A good meal make a special fellowship that can break down barriers. I hope you enjoy the cookbook.

In Memory Of
Goldie V. Young Franklin
Sunrise-0 9 -6 -1912
Sunset-06-24-2009

A Recipe For The Good Life

A heaping cup of Kindness
Two cups of love and caring
One cup of understanding
One cup of joyful sharing

A level cup of patience
One cup of thoughtful insight
One cup of gracious listening
One cup of sweet forgiveness

Mix ingredients together
Toss in smiles and laughter
Serve to everyone you know
With love forever after.

In Memory of

GOLLIE V. YOUNG FRANKLIN LIL MAMA

09-6-12

CJ's Appetizer

Strawberries are red
Blueberries are blue
Pickles are green
Spread your lettuce
And sauce make you scream

Salad is just mayo
Add the bread
Subtract the cucumbers
Divide the avocados
And hope you don't multiply

Don't ask me no questions
I won't tell a lie
You ask me again
I might have to appetizer.

Old-Fashioned Tea Cake

2 cup flour

1 cup sugar

¼ cup peanut butter

3 eggs

¼ tsp. baking powder

1 tsp. nutmeg

¼ tsp. vanilla extract

¼ tsp. salt

Cream the wet ingredients together, then add the dry ingredients into the bowl and mix well. Form the dough Into three 2-inch thick roll and wrap in waxed paper. Chill for 3 hours, then slice in ¼-inch thick slices and place on baking sheet. Bake at 350 degrees for 10 minutes, then Sprinkle with cinnamon sugar.

Charlotte Mold

1 tbsp. unflavored gelatin	4 egg whites
¼ cup pineapple juice	¾ cup sugar
¼ cup boiling water	2 cup pineapples
2 cup heavy cream, whopped	¼ cup wine

Soften the gelatin in cold pineapple juice, add the boiling water and stir until dissolved. Add the wine and cool. Beat the egg whites until soft peaks form. Beat until stiff peaks form, adding ½ cup sugar Add remaining sugar to whipped cream, then add pineapple, fold in egg white. Fold in the gelatin and pour into a mold. Refrigerate for 2 hour or until firm.

Celest Fig Bread

2 cup flour

1 cup sugar

½ cup butter

½ cup milk

1 cup figs

1 tbsp. baking powder

1 tsp. salt

1 tsp. poppy seed

2 eggs

½ cup pecans

Preheat oven to 375 degrees. Into a large bowl, add the wet ingredients mix well. Into a medium bowl, add the dry ingredients and mix. Pour the dry mixture into wet and mix well. Pour fig mixture into a greased loaf pan. Bake for 50 minutes or brown.

Salmon Pie

1 lb. salmon(diced)

1 cup cream of shrimp

½ cup light cream

½ lb. broccoli(diced)

¼ tsp. onion powder

½ cup cream cheese

2 egg white

1 tbsp. lemon juice

1 tsp. old bay seasoning

¼ tsp. dill weed

½ cup butter

¼ tsp. garlic powder

½ cup almond(sliced)

1 pie crust

In a large bowl, combine all the ingredients and mix well. Pour the mixture into the pie crust. Cover with top pie crust and cut in center. Bake at 350 degrees for 30 minutes.

Strawberries Banana cake

2 cup flour

1 cup sugar

1 cup bananas

½ cup butter

1 cup strawberries

½ cup sour cream

3 eggs

1 tbsp. Cake spice

1 tsp. strawberry extract

1 tsp. Banana extract

¼ tsp. Salt

1 tbsp. baking powder

1 tbsp. Lemon juice

1 tsp. Lemon zest

In a large bowl cut up strawberries and bananas and mash. Add the wet ingredients. Then mix up the dry ingredients. Pour the wet into the dry ingredients mix together Pour the mixture into grease and flour Bundt pan. Bake at 350 degree for 30 minutes. Remove from pan and let cool completely.

Sweet Potato Pie

6 Sweet potatoes   ½cup brown sugar

1 tsp. Cinnamon   ½ tsp. Salt

1 tsp. Ginger   2 cup milk

1 tsp. Nutmeg   3 eggs

1 tsp. Vanilla extract   ½ cup butter

1 unbaked pie crust

Preheat the oven 350 degrees. Boil sweet potatoes until tender Peel and mash sweet potatoes, and put into a large bowl. Combine all ingredients and mix well. Pour the sweet potatoes mixture into a unbaked pie crust. Bake for 40 minutes to 1 hour

Mango Roast Chicken

1 chicken

¼ cup mango nectar

¼ tsp. Onion powder

1 cup celery chopped

¼ cup garlic powder

¼ cup oil

1 cup red onion chopped

1 cup mango chopped

1 tsp. salt

1 tsp. Pepper

1/3 cup brown sugar

1 cup bell pepper chopped

½ cup corn syrup

¼ tsp. ground ginger

¼ cup chicken broth

Combine the chopped mango, celery, bell pepper, red onion, oil in a bowl and toss lightly to blend. Place in cavity of chicken with mango mixture, then tie chicken legs with string to hold close to body. Place the chicken on rack in a roasting pan and add chicken broth. Cover, bake at 375 degrees for 1 hour. Combine remaining oil with remaining ingredients. Uncover chicken and brush with half of the mango mixture. Then put back into the oven for 30 minutes. Then brushing frequently with remaining mango mixture.

Pretzels Tart

2 cup pretzels	½ cup pine nuts
5 lb. ground chicken	½cup onion
2 lb. spinach leaves	1/3 cup garlic
1 cup diced tomatoes	½ cup bell pepper
½ cup butter	¼ tsp. nutmeg
2 cup cheese	¼ tsp. chicken seasoning
1/3 cup canola oil	2 tbsp. parsley
¼ cup sour cream	¼ tsp. cumin
¼ cup heavy cream	3 tbsp. sugar

Combine sugar pine nuts with pretzels in a food processor. Slowly add the butter, processing until well blended. Press The crumbs into the bottom tart pan- Heat the oven to 350 degree. Bake the crust for 10 minutes, cool before filling the crust will harden as it cools. Brown the ground chicken, onion, garlic, bell pepper in canola oil in a large skillet, then add spice. Add the spinach and cook for 3 minutes, stirring frequently. Add the tomatoes, cheese, add remaining ingredients. Pour the mixture into tart pan. Bake for 20minutes at 350 degrees.

Fritos Pie

2 cup Fritos

1 lb. ground beef

1/3 cup chili sauce

½ cup diced tomatoes

¼ cup bell pepper

1 cup red beans

¼ cup onion

¼ cup garlic

¼ tsp. chili powder

¼ tsp. brown sugar

¼ tsp. oregano

¼ tsp. parsley flakes

Sauté the beef until partially done. Add the vegetables and cook until brown. In a large bowl add the remaining ingredients. Pour the beef and vegetables into the bowl mix together. In a baking dish greased and add the Fritos to the bottom. Pour the mixture on top of the Fritos, then add the cheese on top. Bake at 350 degree for 20 minutes.

Pear Cream Pie

4 cup pear(sliced)

½ cup sweetened milk

½ cup heavy cream

1 cup cream cheese

1/3 cup sugar

¼ cup flour

1 tbsp.pie spice

1 tsp. vanilla extract

¼ tsp. salt

4 tbsp. butter

3 eggs

1 graham cracker crust

Combine the milk and cream and butter in a large bowl mix well. Add all the ingredients into the bowl mix well. Pour the mixture into pie crust. Bake at 350 degree for 20 minutes.

Throw Together Cake

2 cup flour

1 cup sugar

2 eggs

¼ cup walnut

1 tsp. vanilla extract

1 tbsp. baking powder

1 tbsp. orange zest

1 tbsp. cake spice

Preheat oven to 350 degrees. Grease and flour cake pan. In a large bowl, stir together the wet ingredient. In a medium bowl add all the dry ingredient. Mix the dry and wet ingredient together. Pour the mixture in cake pan. Bake for 30 minutes.

Crab Stuffing

2 cup crabmeat

2 cup stuffing mix

1 cup shredded cheese

¼ cup onion

¼ cup garlic

¼ cup celery

¼ tsp. salt &pep per

¼ tsp. lemon juice

½ cup ranch mix

1/3 cup milk

1 tsp. dry mustard

1 tbsp. old bay seasoning

Place the crabmeat in a bowl. Cook the onion, garlic, celery in oil over low heat until tender. Add all the ingredient in with crab and stirring frequently, serve.

Plantain Pie

4 plantain	1 tbsp. lemon juice
½ cup brown sugar	¼ tsp. Cardamom
½ cup sugar	¼ tsp. cinnamon
½ cup butter	¼ tsp. mace
1/3 cup heavy cream	¼ tsp. nutmeg
2 eggs	1 tbsp. almond extract
½ cup almond	¼ tsp. ginger
¼ cup banana nectar	1 pie crust

Peel plantain and mash. Combine all the ingredient in a large bowl and mix well. Pour the mixture into pie crust Bake at 350 degree for 30 minutes.

Pina Colada Shake

1cup ice cream

1cup crushed ice

½cup pineapple crushed

1/3cup pineapple juice

½cup coconut powder

1/3cup coconut milk

¼cup sugar syrup

3/4cup rum

Combine all ingredients in a blender and whiz until smooth. Pour shake into a glass. Serve.

Seafood Rice

2 cup scallops

2 cup shrimp[chopped]

2 cup crab[can]

2 cup rice

1 tbsp. Parsley[dry]

1 cream cheese[package]

1 cream of shrimp

1 tsp. curry

1 tsp-old-bay

seasons

¼ cup green onion

1 cup celery[chopped]

Cook the rice 10 minutes or done. In a pot then Bring to a boil shrimp, scallops until tender. In a large bowl combine all the ingredients and Mix-well. Add the rice and mix lightly. Serve.

Sucidial Wings

15 chicken wings

½ cup hot sauce

1/3 cup chili oil

½ cup chili sauce

¼ cup Worcestershire Sauce

1/3 cup jalapeno pepper

1 tbsp. brown sugar

1 tbsp. honey

1 tsp. cayenne pepper

1 tsp. chipotle pepper

1 tsp. chili powder

1 tsp. allspice

¼ tsp. lemon pepper

Preheat oven at 350 degrees. Soak the wings in beer overnight. In a large bowl add the ingredient and mix well. Bake the wings 30 minutes. Then pour the mixture over the wings. serve

Rutabagas Casseroles

4 cup rutabagas

2 cup zucchini

½ cup butter

¼ cup sour cream

1 cup cheese(cheddar)

¼ cup Italian seasoning

¼ tsp. salt

¼ tsp. cayenne pepper

¼ tsp. nutmeg

1 tsp. sugar

¼ cup milk

¼ tsp. cornstarch

Peel, slice and put the rutabagas and zucchini in water bring to a boil until tender. Drained. In a large bowl mash rutabagas and zucchini and add remaining ingredients mix well. Pour the mixture in a greased baking dish on the top add remaining cheddar cheese bake at 350 degrees for 20 minutes.

Lilmama Cobbler

2 cup strawberry

2 cup blueberry

2 cup raspberry

2 cup blackberry

½ cup sugar

1 tsp. allspice

1 tsp. cardamom

¼ cup cornstarch

½ cup butter

4 cup cranberry juice

Dumplings

2 cup flour

1 tbsp. baking powder

½ cup butter

1 cup sugar

½ cup milk

1 tbsp. vanilla powder

Wash the berries and place into baking pan. Combine the sugar, cornstarch and allspice, cardamom in a pot and stir in reserved juice slowly, cook over medium heat, stirring, until thickened. Cool, pour into baking pan over berries and dot with butter. Combine the dry ingredient mix-well. Then stir in the wet ingredient and mix together. And drop by tablespoonfuls into baking pan. Bake at 350 degrees for 50 minutes or until done.

Oprah Salad

1 cup oranges mandarin

1 cup pears

1 cup raspberries

1 cup apples

1 tbsp. Honey

¼ tsp. chilli powder

1 cup spinach

¼ tsp. cumin

½ cup walnut

1 tbsp. Vinegar

1 tbsp. Canola oil

¼ cup cream cheese

In a bowl combine the fruit and spinach, walnut and seasoning toss together. Mix dressing and serve.

Watermelon Shake

2 cup watermelon

2 cup ice cream

¼ cup lime soda

¼ cup simple syrup

Combine all ingredients in a blender and whiz until smooth. Cut the watermelon into cube.

Shawn Raspberry Tea

8 tea bags

4 cup water

1cup raspberry

1 cup sugar

½ cup gin

¼ tsp. peppermint extract

1 tbsp. lemon juice

2 cup ginger ale

In a large pot. Add 4 cup of water and tea bags. Let tea come to a boil. Remove the tea bags, Into a small pot add Sugar, water and raspberry let the sugar dissolved. Then allow the mixture to cool. Pour the syrup into the tea. And add the ginger ale, and gin, and stir the tea. Serve.

Annie's Hawaiian Punch

1 large can pineapple

1 large can cranberry juice

1 quart of orange juice

1 large bottle of 7up

1 cup sugar

Mix all ingredients together in a large pitcher.

CJ'S Lemonade

2 cup lemon juice

2 cup water

1 cup sugar

½ cup lemon liqueur

2 cup lemon slices

¼ tsp. Peppermint extract

In a large pitcher mix the ingredients together. Add the ice cubes and servings.

Mama's Vanilla Shake

2 cup vanilla ice cream

½ cup vanilla syrup

1 cup milk

½ cup heavy cream

All the ingredients in a blender. Turn to low speed. Pour in a glass and serving.

CJ'S Fruits Smoothie

1 cup banana

1 cup mango

1 cup blackberry

½ cup orange juice

¼ cup syrup

1 cup raspberry

1 cup peach

1 cup pineapple

2 cup ice cubes

Add all the ingredients into blender and blend until smooth. Serve.

CJ'S Hot Chocolate

½ cup milk   ¼ tsp.cinnamon

½ cup heavy cream   1/3 cup cocoa powder

1 cup sugar   1 tsp. vanilla extract

½ cup marshmallow   ¼ cup chocolate liqueur

Combine all ingredients in a pot bring to a boil. Stirring constantly for 5 minutes. Pour in cup with marshmallow on top. Servings.

Fruits Shake

1 cup watermelon

1 cup mango

½ cup milk

2 cup ice cube

1 cup ice cream

¼ cup vodka

In a blender add all ingredients. Turn the speed to low until smooth. Pour the shake into a glass. Serve.

Hot Mocha

½ cup cocoa

½ cup dry milk

½ cup water

½ tsp. instant coffee

1 cup sugar

½ cup heavy cream

Bring water to a boiling then pour all the ingredients stir the mix well. Pour into mug, In a bowl add the cream and sugar and stir until the cream become thick. On top with whipped topping.

Honey And Pineapple

½ cup honey

1 butter[sticks]

2 tbsp. soy sauce

½ cup brown sugar

½ cup pineapple chopped

½ cup pineapple juice

Combine all ingredients in a bowl and brush on Turkey. Basting frequently with glaze mixture. Bake for about 15minutes,

Cranberry Glazed

1 cup cranberry

1 tsp. onion powder

1/3 cup orange juice

1 tbsp. Molasses

1/3 tsp. salt

1 tsp. oil

1 tsp. garlic powder

1tbsp.brown sugar

1 tsp. jalapeno juice

1 tbsp. red wine vinegar

In a small pot put all ingredient heat up the mixture. To medium-low heat for 10 to 15minutes.

Chicken gravy

1 cream of chicken

1 tsp. salt

1 cup. Chicken stock

1 tsp. pepper

3 tbsp. margarine

1 tsp. sage powder

1 tbsp. kitchen bouquet

1 tsp. poultry powder

¼ tsp. garlic powder

1 tsp. onion powder

Combine the cream of chicken .stock, and margarine in a saucepan and heat. Add all ingredients to the saucepan stirring constantly, until margarine are melted. Pour over chicken. Bake for 20 minutes.

Mongo Sauce

2 cup mango juice

1 tbsp. lemon juice

½ cup brown sugar

1 tsp. onion powder

1 tsp. cayenne pepper

1 tsp. ginger

1 tbsp. Worcestershire

1 tbsp. corn starch

½ cup orange juice

½ tbsp. vinegar[white]

1/3 cup sugar

1 tsp. garlic powder

1 tsp. nutmeg

1 tsp. mustard[dry]

½ cup corn syrup

2 tbsp. oil

Combine all of the ingredients in a large pot and bring over heat. Stirring occasionally for at least one hours, and use after cool.

Beef Pot Pie

1 lb. beef ground	2 tbsp. onion powder
1 mix vegetable [package]	1 tsp. garlic powder
½ cup bell pepper[chopped]	1 tsp. paprika
¼ cup cheese [grated]	½ cup milk
¾ cup cornmeal	¾ cup flour
3 tbsp. water	1 tsp. salt
	3 tbsp. oil

Sift flour, cornmeal and 1 tsp. salt together into a mixing Bowl. Add in ½ cup shortening, Combine 6 tbsp. milk and Water and stir into the flour mixture. Roll out ¾ of the Pastry on a floured board and line pie pan. Bake at 425 Degrees for 10 minutes. brown the ground beef and bell Pepper over low heat in 3 tbsp. oil add the seasons Remaining vegetable, cheese and mix thoroughly Remove from heat. Add ½ cup milk and pour into bake crust. Roll out remaining pastry, place over pie Bake for 15 minutes or until brown. Serve

Chicken Pot Pie

1 package peas	4 cup chicken [chopped]
1 package broccoli	2 cup cream
1 package carrots	½ tsp. salt
1 cream of chicken	½ tsp. Pepper
1 cup cheese	2 pie crust
2 cup chicken stock	1 tsp. onion powder
½ cup celery	¼cup butter

Place the chicken in a large pot. Cook the chicken For 40minute. Remove chicken from broth. Cool. Cut the chicken up in pieces. Place in a large bowl Combine the mixture in with the chicken mix-well. Pour the filling in the pie crust. Cove the top of the pie And seal edge of pie crust. Cut several slashed in the top To allow steam to escape. Bake at 400 degrees for 30 To 40 minutes or until crust is brown.

Apple Pie

4 cup apple

½ tsp. cinnamon

2 tbsp. lemon juice

2 tbsp. butter

1 cup sugar

¼ tsp. mace

2 tbsp. cornstarch

¼ tsp. nutmeg

¼ tsp. apple spice

½ cup cream

Peel apple and cut into small pieces. Place in a large bowl. Add the spice and cornstarch and cream. Pour the mixture into the pie shell. Bake at 375 degrees for 40 minutes.

Banana Pie

6 banana[mash]

¼ cup baking mix

1 cup sugar

3 eggs

½ cup sour cream

Pie shell

1 tbsp. banana extract

½ cup butter

¼ tsp. salt

½ cup cream cheese

½ cup cream

Mix 1 cup sugar, baking mix and salt in top of a double Boiler, And stir in small amount of the cream sour cream And cream cheese Stir in remaining cream and cook over boiling water stirring, until thick cover and cook for 10 minutes longer, stirring occasionally add small of the hot Mixture to beaten egg yolks. Stir back into hot mixture and Cook for 10 minutes longer. Add butter and banana extract And stir until butter is melted. Place the bananas in the pie Shell and pour filling over bananas. Cool slightly beat the egg white in a bowl until stiff, adding remaining sugar gradually. Spread over filling. Bake at 350 degrees for 15 minutes or brown.

Nutcracker Pie

1 cup pecan	½ cup sugar
1 cup almond	½ cup brown sugar
1 cup walnut	1 cup corn syrup
1 cup chestnut	¼ cup butter
1 tsp. cinnamon	1 tbsp. vanilla extract
1 tsp. nutmeg	3 eggs
½ tsp. allspice	1 pie shell

Beat eggs, spice and sugars together. Stir in syrup vanilla And butter. Place nuts on the bottom of the pie shell and Cove with mixture. Bake 45minutes or center comes out Clean.

Shawn Lemon Pie

¼ cup sugar

½ cup lemon juice

1/3 cup cornstarch

½ cup water

1 tbsp. lemon extract

2 tsp. lemon zest

2 tbsp. butter

2 eggs yolks

In a small pot combine all the ingredients and cook Stirring frequently, until smooth and thick 15minutes. Turn off the heat, then let the mixture cool. Pour into The pie crust.

The Meringue

2 tbsp. lemon juice

2 tbsp. lemon zest

2 eggs white

¼ tsp. cream of tartar

¼ cup powder sugar

1/3 tsp. salt

Beat the egg whites with cream of tartar in a bowl until Foamy. Add all the ingredients with the mixture. And Spread overfilling sealing to crust. Bake at 325degrees for 15minutes or until brown. Cool.

Peanut Butter Pie

½ cup peanut butter

½ cup brown sugar

½ cup cream cheese

½ cup cream

1/3 cup pudding mix

½ tsp. Allspice

½ cup butter

1 tbsp. vanilla extract

2 eggs

½ cup corn syrup

1 cup chestnut

½ tsp. pie spice

Combine the eggs and peanut butter and mix until Well blended. Combine the ingredient and blend into the mixture. Pour the mixture into the pie crust. Bake at 350 degrees for 1 hour

Breakfast Pie

1 lb. chorizo

1 lb. Italian sausage

2 cup potatoes(shredded)

1 cup mozzarella cheese

1 cup cheddar cheese

1 cup zucchini(shredded)

6 eggs

½ cup heavy cream

¼ tsp.dill weed

¼ tsp. parsley

¼ cup onion

¼ cup garlic

¼ tsp. accent

¼ tsp. hot sauce

½ cup butter

¼ tsp. celery flaked

Peel potatoes and zucchini in a food processor shredded one at a time. In a skillet brown the chorizo, sausage remove the meat and sauté the vegg. Pour the meat and vegg into a bowl add all the ingredients except the potatoes Mix well. Place the shredded potatoes at the bottom of pie pan. Pour the mixture in the pan and add the cheeses on top. Bake at 350 degree for 45 minutes or until the center come out clean. Serve

Squash Pie

2 cup squash	½ tsp. Nutmeg
1 cup brown sugar	1 tsp. Cinnamon
½ cup butter	½ tsp. Cloves
1 cup milk	½ tsp. cardamom
3 eggs	½ tsp. ginger
¼ tsp. Salt	1 pie shell

Combine the brown sugar salt spice and squash and mix thoroughly. Add the eggs butter and milk to squash mixture and mix well then pour into pie shell. Preheat the oven 400 degrees and bake for 45 minutes. Allow to cool slightly before serving.

Mango Pie

2 cup mango[sliced]

1 cup mango nectar

½ cup cream

¼ tsp. Salt

Pie crust

2 tbsp. gelatin[unflavored]

¼ cup sugar

1 tsp. almond extract

1 graham cracker

Dissolve the gelatin in hot mango nectar In a bowl. Add cream and salt and sugar and almond extract Stir until mix, Chill for 15 minutes or until syrupy Fold in mangos and pour into pie crust. Chill for 1 Hour.

Pie Crust

¼ cup butter   1 ¼ cup graham cracker

¼ cup sugar

Into a bowl mix the graham cracker and sugar and butter Preheat the oven 350degree and bake for 10 minutes.

Whipped Cream

1 cup cream[heavy]   1/3 cup sugar

1 tbsp. Almond extract

Into a small bowl mix the cream and sugar and almond extract together. Chill for 10 minutes.

Taco Pie

1 lb. fish fillets

4 cup tortilla crumbs

1 cup black bean

2 cup cheese(shredded)

1 cup diced tomatoes

½ cup avocados

2 cup lettuce(shredded)

¼ cup garlic

1/3 cup onion

1 tsp. taco seasoning

1 tsp. old bay seasoning

1/3 cup sour cream

½ cup taco sauce

½ cup butter

Food processor mix tortilla chips with butter to make the crumbs. Press into the pie plate to form a crust. Bake at 350 degrees for 15 minutes. Brown the fish, onion and garlic in the butter skillet. In a bowl add the bean and sauce and spice. Stir in cheese and fish mixture And all the remaining ingredients. Then on top add the lettuce and cheese. serve

Carrot Pie

1 cup pureed carrot

I/2 cup brown sugar

¼ cup maple syrup

½ cup heavy cream

1/3 cup walnuts

1 tbsp. pie spice

1 tsp. poppy seed

¼ tsp. cream of tartar

2 eggs

1 pie crust

Place the carrot puree in a food processor, blend in the sugar, syrup and spices and walnuts. Whip in the eggs, cream of tartar stir until smooth.

Blueberry Pie

¼ cup butter

1 cup coconut powder

¼ cup flour

2 eggs

1 cup sugar

4 cup blueberries

1 tsp. nutmeg

1 tbsp. vanilla extract

¼ tsp. mace

½ cup heavy cream

Wash the blueberries and mash place in a large bowl. Add all ingredient and mix well. Pour the mixture into pie crust. Bake at 350 degree for 30 minutes.

Kiwi Pie

2 cup kiwi

1 cup coconut flake

½ cup almond

½ cup sweetened milk

2 eggs

¼ cup unflavored gelatin

1 tsp. lime juice

¼ tsp. almond extract

1 graham cracker crust

¼ cup sugar

In a bowl mix all ingredients together. Except kiwi, coconut into the crust add the kiwi, coconut at the bottom. Pour the Mixture over the top of kiwi, coconut. Bake at 350 degrees for 20 minutes.

Shepherd's Pie

2 pounds turkey(ground)	¼ cup onion (minced)
2 pounds lamb(ground)	¼ cup garlic(minced)
1 cup Cheddar cheese	¼ cup bell pepper
2 cup broccoli	¼ cup celery
1 cup heavy cream	¼ tsp. marjoram
½ cup butter	¼ tsp. black pepper
2 cup carrots	¼ tsp. salt
2 medium eggplant	¼ tsp. thyme

Boil eggplant and broccoli until lender. Cool. Mash fine. Place vegetables into large skillet on medium heat. Sauté until tender. Add the meat and all the ingredient mix-well. Pour the meat mixture into a bake dish. Spoon the mashed Eggplant on top, covering the mixture completely. Bake at 375 degrees until brown.

Orange Cream Pie

1 cup mandarin orange

½ cup orange juice

½ cup heavy cream

½cup sugar

½ cup ricotta cheese

1/3 cup unflavored gelatin

1 tsp. orange extract

1 tsp. orange food coloring

1 9-in pie crust

½ cup cream cheese

Drain the orange and blend in a food processor in a small bowl add the gelatin on the cold orange juice. Pour gelatin Into the food processor and acid all the ingredients together mix. Pour the mixture into pie crust refrigerate for 1 hour or until firm.

Pinto Bean Pie

2 cup pinto beans

½ cup flour

1 cup cream cheese

1/3 cup heavy cream

1 cup brown sugar

¼ cup butter(melted)

1 tsp. baking powder

1 tbsp. pie spice

¼ tsp. vanilla extract

2 eggs

¼ cup ginger paste

1 9-in pie crust

In a food processor mix all the wet ingredients together. Blend in the mashed pinto beans then add the dry ingredient mix well. Pour the mixture into a pie crust. Bake 350 degrees until firm.

Avocados Cream Pie

2 cup avocados

1 cup s.c. milk

1 cup cream cheese

¼ cup flour

½ cup butter

4 drops of green Food coloring

¼ cup lime juice

¼ cup sugar

¼ tsp. vanilla extract

¼ tsp. pie spice

2 eggs

1 egg whites

¼ tsp. cream of tartar

Blend the avocados and cream cheese and lime juice into the food processor until smooth, add all the remaining ingredients to the food processor mix well. Pour the mixture to the pie crust. Bake at 350 degrees for 20 minutes.

Strawberry-Banana Pie

2 cup strawberry

2 cup banana

1 cup cream cheese

1 cup whipped cream

1 cup sugar

1/3 cup lemon juice

1/3 cup strawberry gelatin

¼ cup butter(melted)

1 graham cracker pie crust

¼ cup corn syrup

Stir gelatin into 1/3 cup cold water In a large bowl mash banana and strawberry together Pour the gelatin into the banana mixture. Add all the ingredient into the mix well. Graham cracker crumbs into a bowl add the butter and sugar mix well. Pour the mixture into the crust Chill for 3 hour.

Oatmeal & Hazelnut Pie

1 cup oatmeal

½ cup brown sugar

½ cup com syrup

2 eggs

½ cup hazelnuts spread

¼ cup hazelnuts

1/3 cup butter

1 tbsp. vanilla extract

Combine all the ingredients and mix-well. Pour the oatmeal mixture into pie crust. Bake at 350degrees for 20minutes.

Oatmeal-nut Pie Crust

1 cup oatmeal   ¼ cup hazelnuts

¼ cup brown sugar   1/3 cup butter (melted)

Into a large bowl combine all the ingredients mix together. Pour the mixture pie pan. Press the side and bottom of a pie pan. Bake at 350 degrees for 10 minutes.

Rum Pie

¼ cup rum   ½ cup wheat flour

½ cup brown sugar   ½ cup heavy cream

2 tsp. unflavored gelatin   ¼ tsp. Cinnamon

¼ cup butter(melted)   ¼ tsp. Nutmeg

3 eggs   1 graham cracker crust

Mix the rum and gelatin in a bowl. Add the rest of the wet ingredient and mix-well. Into a small bowl add all dry ingredient. Pour the dry into the wet mix together. Pour the mixture in the pie shell Bake at 350 degrees for 20 minutes.

Cherry Pie

2 cup cherry(mash)

1 cup sugar

½ cup heavy cream

½ cherry gelatin

1 graham cracker pie crust

¼ tsp. pie spice

2 tbsp. cornstarch

1 tsp. vanilla extract

¼ cup red food coloring

In a large bowl mash the cherry. Drain the cherries juice add alt ingredient except gelatin and mix-well. Into a small bowl add cool water and gelatin mix well. Pour the gelatin in the mixture stir. Pour the mixture into pie crust and chill.

Coconut Pie

1 cup coconut flaked	1 tsp. coconut extract
1 cup sugar	¼ tsp. pie spice
½ cup coconut milk	¼ cup pudding mix
½ cup butter	1 pie crust
3 eggs	1 tbsp. vinegar

Cream the eggs and sugar together Acid all ingredient and mix-well. Pour into the pie crust. Bake at 350 degrees for 45 minutes.

Carolyn Jean Franklin Allen

Coconut Crust

1 cup coconut flaked   ¼ cup butter

½ cup vanilla wafer crumbs   ¼ cup sugar

Combine the coconut mixture with melted butter and sugar. Press firmly against the bottom and the side. Chill for 1 hour or until firm.

Cocoa Cream Pie

½ cup chocolate chips

1 cup chocolate syrup

1 cup marshmallows

1 cup heavy cream

2 eggs

½ tsp. almond extract

¼ cup cornstarch

½ cup corn syrup

½ cup almonds

1 pie shell

Heat the cream in a pot. Add the marshmallows and stir until melted. Add all the ingredients in the marshmallows mixture. Pour the mixture into the pie shell. Chill until firm.

Oatmeal Pie

2 cup oatmeal

1 cup peach

½ cup raisins

4 eggs

1 cup heavy cream

1 cup brown sugar

1 tbsp. pie spice

½ butter(stick)

1 tsp. vanilla extract

½ cup peach

¼ cup honey

1 unbaked pie shell

Combine the wet ingredients and beat well. Stir in the oats, raisins, pecans, pour the mixture into the pie shell. Bake at 350 degrees for 30 minutes.

Watermelon Pie

2 cup watermelon

1 cup sugar

1/3 cup watermelon Gelatin

¼ cup vinegar

2 tbsp. red food coloring

2 tbsp. cornstarch

I tsp. pie spice

¼ tsp. salt

¼ tsp. peppermint extract

1 graham cracker crust pie

Soften the gelatin in ¼ cup watermelon juice in a small bowl. Cut the green rind off the watermelon. Place in a saucepan and cover with water. Cook until tender, then drain. Add remaining ingredients into the bowl with gelatin add the watermelon to the mixture. Bake at 350 degrees for 30 minutes or until clone.

Pineapple Pie

1 cup crushed pineapple

½ cup sweetened milk

½ cup crushed mango

1/3 cup pineapple gelatin

2 eggs yolks

1 tbsp. lemon juice

¼ tsp. accent powder

¼ tsp. pie spice

2 tbsp. sugar

¼ cup cream cheese

Dissolve the gelatin in liquid in a bowl. Blend the milk, lemon juice, eggs yolk and sugar together, then fold in the pineapple and mango. Pour into pie shell. Bake at 350 degrees for 20 minutes or until browned.

Eggnog cheese cake

4 cream cheese [package]   4 eggs

1 cup sour cream   2 eggs {yolks}

2 tsp. vanilla extract   ¼ tsp salt

¼ tsp. almond extract   1 cup milk

1½ cup sugar   2 tbsp. nutmeg

1 cup whipping cream   3 tbsp. butter [melted]

Combine all ingredients in a large bowl. Mix-well fold in the whipping cream.
Pour into pie shell bake at 400 degrees for 40 minutes or until golden cool.

Cranberry Cake

2 cup flour	½cup orange juice
1 cup brown sugar	¼ tsp. allspice
1 cup sugar	¼ tsp. mace
1 cup cranberry jelly	¼ tsp. cardamom
3 eggs	1 tbsp. vanilla extract
½ cup butter	¼ tsp. nutmeg

Combine all dry ingredient into a large bowl. Into a Large bowl. Into a small bowl wet ingredient. Pour the wet into the dry ingredient mix together. Pour the Mixture into the bund pan. Bake at 350 degree for 45 minutes.

LILMAMA
Layer coconut Cake

4 cup cake flour

3 cup sugar

1 cup butter

1 cup coconut milk

2 cup coconut flaked

1 tbsp. baking powder

5 eggs

1 tsp. salt

1 tsp. vanilla extract

1 tsp. coconut extract

Preheat the oven to 350 degrees. Butter and flour cake pan. Combine dry ingredient into a large bowl. All the wet ingredient mix together. Pour the wet into the dry ingredient and mix well. Pour the mixture into the cakes pan. Bake for 1 hour. Bake the coconut flaked until lightly toasted 10 minutes.

Coconut Cream Cheese Icing

4 pkg. cream cheese; softened   1 tbsp. milk

½ cup butter   4 cup powder sugar

1 tsp. coconut extract

Combine all ingredients beat until smooth. Use on cake, On top of the icing put the toasted coconut.

Sock To Me Cake

2 cup cake flour	1 tbsp. baking powder
1 cup sugar	1 tsp. salt
½ cup brown sugar	½ cup butter
3 eggs	1 tbsp. vanilla extract
1 cup sour cream	1 tsp. nutmeg
¼ cup cream[heavy]	½ cup pecans

Into a large bowl add all dry ingredient into a small bowl Add all wet ingredient mix well. Pour the wet ingredient into dry and mix. Pour the mixture into baking pan. Bake at 350 Degree. Bake for 30minutes.

Glaze

1/3 cup powder sugar   3 tbsp. milk

1 tbsp. vanilla extract   ¼ cup pecan

Combine all the ingredients into a bowl mix. Pour on top of the cake.

Oatmeal Cake

2 cup flour

½ cup brown sugar

½ cup sugar

½ cup butter

2 cup oatmeal

1 cup milk

2 eggs

1 tsp. almond extract

1 tsp. vanilla extract

½ cup raisins

½ cup almond

1 tbsp. baking powder

Sift the dry ingredient into a bowl, whisk the wet ingredient together. Pour the wet into the dry mix-well. Preheat the oven 375 degrees. Grease the cake pan Pour the mixture into the cake pan. Bake for 30minutes.

Prune Cake

2 cup flour

2 cup sugar

1 cup butter milk

3 eggs

1 cup prunes

1¼ cup pecan

1 cup oil

1 tbsp. cinnamon

1 tbsp. Nutmeg

1 tbsp. Allspice

1 tbsp. cloves

¼ tsp. salt

1 tbsp. Baking powder

2 tbsp. Vanilla extract

Combine ail ingredient in large bowl mix well alternately Add the wet ingredient mix. Mash prunes with fork. Add Prunes and pecans to batter. Bake in a greased bund pan at 350 degree for 1 hour.

Chocolate Cake

2 cup cake flour

1 cup brown sugar

½ cup sugar

5 eggs

1 cup chocolate chips

1 cup butler

1/3 cup sour cream

¼ cup liqueur chocolate

½ cup cream[heavy]

½ cup cocoa powder

1 tsp. cardamom

1 tsp. Vanilla extract

Preheat oven 350 degrees. Grease the cake pan with oil and cocoa powder. Sift dry ingredient into large bowl add the wet ingredient into the dry ingredient mix together. Pour the mixture into Cake pan. Bake for 1 hour.

Rice Cake

1 cup rice flour

1/3 cup rice

½ cup butter

1/3 cup heavy cream

½ cup sugar

1 cup puree mango

1 tbsp baking powder

1 tsp. vanilla extract

¼ tsp. salt

¼ tsp. turmeric

¼ tsp. cinnamon

2 egg whites

Cook the rice in the water until tender. Puree the mango pour into a large bowl. Add the remaining ingredient into the bowl. Add the rice to the mixture. Mix together well. Pour the mixture into a cake pan. Bake at 350 degrees. For 15 to 20 minutes.

Bonnies Chocolate Tea Cake

½ cup butter

½ cup sugar

½ cup cocoa powder

¼ tsp. salt

1 cup flour

¼ cup molasses

2 eggs

2 tsp. baking powder

½ cup brown sugar

¼ tsp. baking soda

1 tsp. vanilla [extract]

¼ cup milk

¼ tsp. Nutmeg

½ cup wheat flour

In and small bowl add all the wet mixture. In a large Bowl add all the dry mixture. Pour the wet mixture In the dry mixture, and mix-well. Bake at 350 degrees 15minutes.

Peanut Butter Cake

2 cup flour

1 cup sugar

½ cup brown sugar

½ cup milk

½cup almond [chopped]

1 tbsp. vanilla [extract]

½ cup peanut butter

½ cup hazelnut

3 eggs

½ cup butter

1 tbsp. almond[extract]

1 ginger

In a bowl melted hazelnut, peanut butter. Sift dry Ingredients together into a bowl. Add the wet ingredients in the bowl and mix well. Bake at 350degree for 1 hour. Cool.

CJ'S Spice Cake

1 cup wheat flour

1 cup flour

1 cup sugar

½ cup brown sugar

4 eggs

1/3 cup sour cream

¼ cup coca powder

1 cup heavy cream

1 tsp. rum[extract]

½ cup butter

1 tbsp. baking powder

1 tsp. cinnamon

1 tsp. cardamom

½ tsp. cloves

½ tsp. allspice

½ tsp. ginger

½ tsp. nutmeg

1 tbsp. vanilla[extract]

In a small bowl wet ingredients and mix. In a large Bowl sift dry ingredients together. Pour the wet ingredients into the dry ingredients and mix. Grease And flour the cake pan. Pour the mixture into cake pan, Bake at 350 degrees for 45minutes. cool

Lilmama Tea Cake

2 cup flour

1 cup sugar

½ cup brown sugar

½ cup butter

2 cup cream cheese

½ cup cream[heavy]

3 eggs

1 tbsp. baking powder

¼ tsp. baking soda

¼ tsp. salt

1 tbsp. vanilla extract

1 tsp. cinnamon powder

1 tsp. nutmeg

1 tsp. allspice

Cream the wet ingredients together, then add the dry ingredients. Beat until well mixed. Form the dough into three 2-inch thick rolls and wrap in waxed paper. Chill For 3 hours, then slice in ¼-inch thick slices and place On baking sheet. Bake at 350 degrees for 10 minutes Then sprinkle with cinnamon sugar.

Cheese Pound Cake

½ cup ricotta cheese

½ cup cream cheese

2 cup flour

½ cup sour cream

1 cup sugar

4 eggs

½ cup butter

1 tbsp. baking powder

¼ tsp. salt

½ tsp. nutmeg

1 tbsp. vanilla extract

½ tsp. allspice

Cream together butter, sugar, salt mix well. Add eggs, one at a time beating well after each addition. Alternately add sour cream, cream cheese, vanilla extract. Mix well stir in the flour, spice mix well. Pour the mixture into greased and floured loaf pan. Bake at 325 degrees for 60 minutes.

FISH CAKE

4 cup halibut fish

½ cup ranch dressing

1 tbsp. Dijon mustard

1 tbsp. parsley

1 tbsp. basil

2 cup bread crumbs

1 egg

1½ tsp. old bay seasoning

1 tsp. oregano

¼ tsp. black pepper

2 tbsp. olive oil

¼ tsp. dill

1 cup parmesan cheese

¼ tsp. Paprika

Combine the wet ingredients into a large bowl. Add the seasoning and fish, add enough bread crumbs to make the fish mixture easy to handle and shape into patties. Bake at 375degrees for 30 minutes or until brown.

Lemon Cake

2 cup flour

1 cup sugar

½ cup butter

1 cup sour cream

1 tbsp. lemon zest

1 tsp. Lemon extract

¼ cup lemon juice

¼ tsp. salt

In a small bowl add wet ingredients mix. In a large bowl add dry ingredients mix. Pour the wet mixture into the dry mix together Pour the mixture into a greased and flour bundt pan. Bake at 350 degree for 40 minutes.

Chocolate-Apple Cake

2 cup wheat flour

1 cup brown sugar

4 eggs

½ cup sour cream

½ cup walnut

½ cup cocoa powder

½ cup butter

1 cup apple

1 tbsp. cake spice

1 tbsp. vanilla extract

¼ tsp. salt

1 tsp. baking powder

1 tsp. baking soda

1/3 cup milk

In a large bowl cream the wet ingredients together. Combine the dry ingredients together. Pour the dry Ingredients into the wet ingredient and mix-well. Pour the mixture into bake pan. Bake 350 degrees for 45 minutes.

Red Velvet Cake

2 cup cake flour	½ tsp. baking powder
1 cup brown sugar	½ tsp. baking soda
1 cup buttermilk	1 tsp. vinegar
2 eggs	1 tbsp. vanilla extract
¼ cup red food coloring	2 tbsp. coca powder
½ cup butter	1 tbsp. cake spice
¼ cup chocolate liqueur	¼ tsp. salt

Preheat oven to 350 degrees. Grease and flour two cake pan. Into a large bowl cream all the wet ingredients together. Into a small bowl mix all dry ingredients together. Add the dry into the mixture little by little mix well. Pour the cake mixture into the cake pans. Bake for 40 minutes.

Rum Cake

2 cup cake flour	1 tbsp. baking powder
1 cup sugar	1 tsp. vanilla extract
2 cup blackberry	¼ tsp. salt
4 eggs	¼ tsp. baking soda
½ cup oil	1/3 cup heavy cream
½ cup rum	½ cup pudding mix

Grease and flour sheet pan. Combine all the dry ingredient. Add the wet ingredient into the dry mix well, pour mixture into pan. Bake at 350 degrees for 1 hour.

Glaze

1 cup powder sugar   ¼ cup rum

½cup butter

In a small bowl whisk together all the glaze ingredient. Pour over hot cake. Let cake cool for 30 minutes, then remove from pan.

Apricot Pound Cake

2 cup flour

1 cup sugar

1 cup apricot

½ cup sour cream

2 eggs

¼ tsp. cake spice

½ cup pecans

1 tbsp. baking powder

¼ tsp. salt

½ cup butter

Into a food processor puree the apricot until smooth. Combine all wet ingredient in a bowl. Pour the wet into dry ingredient and mix well. Pour into a greased and flour loaf pan. Bake at 350 degrees for 60 minutes.

Hazelnut Cake

2 cup wheat flour	1 tbsp. baking powder
1 cup brown sugar	¼ tsp. baking soda
4 egg whites	1 tbsp. cake spice
½ cup hazelnut oil	½ cup hazelnut spread
½ cup hazelnut(chopped)	1 tsp. vanilla extract
½ cup sour cream	¼ tsp. Cream of tartar

Sift dry ingredients together and place in a bowl. Into a small bowl add all the wet ingredients together Pour the dry ingredients into the wet and mix-well. Pour the hazelnut mixture into greased and flour cake pan. Bake at 350 degrees. Bake for 30 minutes.

Hazelnut Glaze

½ cup hazelnut liqueur   1cup sugar

1 cup water

Boil 1 cup water and 1 cup sugar together 5 minutes. Add liqueur. When cake has been out of the oven about 10 minutes. Remove it from pan and baste with glaze mixture.

CJ'S 7-Up Cheesecake

2 cup cream cheese   ½ cup butter

1 cup ricotta cheese   1 tbsp. almond extract

1 cup powder sugar   ½ cup sour cream

4 egg whites   1 cup 7-up

1 cup wheat flour   ½ cup almond

Into a large bowl cream all wet ingredients together. Into a small bowl combine all the dry ingredients. Pour all the dry into the wet and mix-well. Pour the mixture into baking dish. Bake 350 degree for 1 hour

Graham Cracker Crust

1½ cup graham cracker   1/3 cup almond

½ cup brown sugar   1/3 cup butter

Combine the crumbs, sugar and almond in a mixing bowl, then blend in the butler. Press firmly the mixture side and bottom of a pie pan. Bake at 350 degrees for 10 minutes or until edges brown slightly. Remove to cooling rack.

Almond Cake

2 cup cake flour	1 tsp. Cardamom
1 cup sugar	1 tsp. cinnamon
½ cup milk	1 tbsp. baking powder
½ cup almond	¼ tsp. salt
½ cup almond butter	1 tsp. almond extract
½ cup butter	4 eggs

Preheat the oven to 350 degrees. Grease and flour bundt pan. Into a large bowl mix all the wet ingredients together. Add the dry little by little until well mix. Pour the mixture into pan bake for 1 hour

Peach cake

2 cup flour	1 tbsp. baking powder
1 cup sugar	¼ tsp. salt
4 cup peach(sliced)	1 tbsp. cake spice
2 cup heavy cream	1 tsp. vanilla extract
1 cup sweetened milk	2 tbsp. peach liqueur
1/3 cup pudding mix	4 eggs

Combine all the wet ingredient in a bowl and mix well. Then add the dry ingredient into the wet and mix together. Pour the peach mixture in a bake pan. Bake at 350 degrees for 1 hour. A toothpick inserted into the center of the cake should come out clean.

Carrot Cake

1 cup flour	1 tsp. baking powder
½ cup sugar	½ tsp. allspice
2 eggs	½ tsp. nutmeg
½ cup butter	½ tsp. mace
½ cup carrots	½ cup pecans
½ cup sour cream	½ cup cream

Into a large bowl add all the wet ingredient together mix well. Into a large add all dry ingredient add all the mixture together mix well. Pour the mixture into a baking pan. Bake for 20 minutes. Preheat oven 350 degrees. Grease flour baking pan.

Fruit Cake

2 cup flour	¼ cup lemon juice
½ cup brown sugar	¼ cup orange zest
½ cup sugar	1 tsp. salt
4 eggs	1 tsp. vanilla extract
½ cup butter	2 tbsp. cocoa powder
1 tbsp. baking powder	1 tsp. cinnamon
½ cup banana	1 tsp. mace powder
½ cup strawberry	1 tsp. nutmeg
½ cup mango	½ cup kiwi
½ cup pear	½ cup peaches
½ cup apple	½ cup pineapple
1/3 cup almond	1/3 cup pecans
1/3 cup walnuts	1/3 cup raisins
¼ cup corn syrup	1/3 cup hazelnut

Preheat oven to 300 degree. Grease and flour bund pan. Combine all fruit into a large bowl. In a large bowl, butter, Eggs, sugar and mix together. Sift all dry ingredient together. Pour all the mixture together and mix well. Pour the mixture into bund pan. Bake for 2 hours.

Pineapple-upside-down Calve

2 cup cake flour	1 tsp. baking powder
1 cup sugar	¼ tsp. salt
1 cup pineapple	1 tsp. vanilla extract
2 eggs	¼ tsp. cake spice
½ cup butter	1 cup pecan(chopped)
½ cup heavy cream	¾ cup brown sugar

Melt butter in a pan and sprinkle the brown sugar oven butter. Spread pineapple over brown sugar. Spread the pecans, over pineapple. Mix dry ingredients together into a bowl. Add the wet ingredients to the dry and mix until smooth. Pour over pineapple mixture. Bake at 350 degrees for 45 minutes. Turn upside down on cake plate and let stand for 10 minutes. Remove from pan and serve.

Seafood Gumbo

1 lb. shrimp

1 lb. crabmeat

1 lb. fish fillets

1 onion[chopped]

1 garlic[minced]

½ cup celery[chopped]

½ lb. okra

1 bell pepper [chopper]

1 tbsp. gumbo file

¼ tbsp. parsley

2 tbsp. roux mix

¼ cup old bay[seasons]

4 cup boiling water shrimp, crabmeat, fish. Combine All the ingredients. Bring to a boil then cove and simmer for 15 to 20minutes. Season with old bay Seasoning. Serve in bowls with rice.

Gumbo

1 lb. chicken

1 lb. sausage

1 lb. shrimp

1 lb. crab

1 lb. okra

1 tbsp. parsley

1 tsp. cayenne pepper

1 chicken broth

1 tbsp. thyme

1 bell pepper[chopped]

1 onion[chopped]

1 garlic[chopped]

1 tbsp. gumbo file

2 tbsp. roux mix

Combine 3 cup water and chicken broth to a boil water Then add all ingredients cove and simmer for 30 minutes. Cook rice separately and pour the gumbo over the rice. serve

Hamburger Soup

1 lb. ground beef

4 cup beef broth

2 cup diced tomatoes

2 cup spinach

1 cup shredded cheese

1/3 cup bell pepper

¼ cup ketchup

½ cup tomato sauce

1 cup bacon(diced)

¼ tsp. salt

¼ tsp. pepper

1 tsp. onion powder

1 tsp. garlic powder

¼ tsp. cumin

1 tsp. parsley

¼ tsp. pickle relish

¼ tsp. dry mustard

½ cup diced jalapeno

In a large skillet Brown ground beef and bacon. Drain. Stir in all the ingredients bring to a boil. Cove and simmer one hour. Serve.

Turkey Soup

2 cup turkey	1 tsp. nutmeg
1 cup carrots	1 tsp. cayenne pepper
1 cup broccoli	1 tsp. cilantro
1 cup cheese	¼ tsp. black pepper
1 cup rice	1 tsp. Cajun
1 cup cream of chicken	1 tsp. curry
1 cup chicken broth	1 tsp. cumin
1 tsp. onion powder	1 tsp. garlic powder
¼ tsp. salt	1 tsp. sugar

Into a large slow cooker, combine all the ingredient. Cover and cook on low 2 hours until soup is done and hot.

Taco Soup

2 cup chorizo(chopped)

1 cup diced tomatoes

½ cup taco sauce

1 cup spinach

½ cup diced avocados

½ cup cream cheese

2 cup com chips(crumbs)

1 tbsp. taco seasoning

1 tsp. onion powder

1tsp. garlic powder

¼tsp. nutmeg

¼tsp.cumin

½cup sour cream

1 cup cheddar cheese

In a skillet brown chorizo in oil. Pour the chorizo mixture in the pot. In a large pot add all the ingredients except corn chips. Bring to a boil. Cook until soup is done. On top corn crumbs and cheese. serve

Crawfish Soup

2 cup crawfish

1 cup potatoes cubed

1 cup corn

2 cup sausage cubed

½ cup heavy cream

½ cup cheese

¼ tsp. cayenne pepper

¼ tsp. coriander

¼ cup onion

¼ cup garlic

1/3 cup fish stock

1 tbsp. Lemon juice

Peeled and cut in cubed potatoes cook for 10 minutes combine all ingredients into low-cooker. Add the potatoes to the low-cooker. Cover and cook for 30 minutes.

Antoinette Shrimp Stew

2 lb. shrimp	1 tsp. parsley
1/3 cup flour	2 tbsp. oil
1 cup potatoes(diced)	1 tbsp. old bay seasoning
2 eggs(hard boil)	¼ cup tomato paste
½ cup bell pepper(chopped)	¼ cup water
½ cup onion(chopped)	½ cup celery(chopped)
½ cup garlic(chopped)	½ diced tomatoes

Sauté the flour, onion, celery, garlic, bell pepper, in the oil until lightly browned in a large skillet. Add the remaining ingredients except the shrimp and simmer for 20 minutes. Add the shrimp and cook for 15minutes. Serve in bowl over rice.

Lilmama's Turtle Stew

2 cup turtle meat

1 cup carrots(diced)

1 cup potatoes(diced)

½ cup bell pepper

½ cup celery

½ cup onion

½ cup garlic

2 cup vegetables stock

2 cup water

1 cup tomatoes(diced)

¼ cup flour

¼ tsp. hot sauce

¼ tsp. marjoram

1 tbsp. lemon juice

½ tsp. mace

¼ tsp.nutmeg

Combine the turtle meat, with ingredient in a large pot, then bring to a boil and cook until the turtle meat is tender.serve

SPINACH SOUP

4 cup spinach

2 cup avocados

1 cup almonds

½cup cream cheese

2 cup chicken stock

1/3 cup sour cream

1/3 cup heavy cream

¼ tsp. nutmeg

¼ tsp. lemon juice

¼ tsp. black pepper

¼ tsp. garlic powder

¼ tsp. onion powder

¼ tsp. Salt

1 tbsp. almond oil

Peel and seed the avocados. Mash the avocados. Place the avocados into low-cook. Add the spinach and all the ingredients to the low-cook. Cook for 30 minutes.

Rabbit Stews

4 lb. rabbit	½cup onion
4 cup water	½cup garlic
½ cup carrots	½ cup celery
½ cup bell pepper	½ tsp. thyme
1 cup heavy cream	¼ tsp. mace
½ cup butter	2 tbsp. lemon juice
1 tsp. paprika	¼ cup soy sauce

Cut the rabbit into serving pieces and place in the low cooker. Add the remaining ingredient on top of the rabbit and cove, Cook until the rabbit is tender, serve.

Chicken Chowder

2 lb. chicken cubed	1 tsp. Cornstarch
1 cup cream of chicken	½ cup onion
1 cup milk	½ cup carrots
½ cup celery	1 bay leaf
2 chicken bouillon cubes	¼ tsp. thyme
1 cup chicken stock	¼ tsp. pepper
1 cup potatoes cubes	1 tbsp. oil

In a large pot, sauté vegetables in oil until tender. Add chicken stock, potatoes, spices, bring to a boil. Cove, Simmer about 15 minutes stir in chicken cubed and milk Stir cornstarch and remaining ingredients. Cook until chowder is thoroughly heated. servings

Lilmama Tomato Soup

4 cup diced tomatoes	1 tsp. onion powder
2 cup heavy cream	1 tsp. garlic powder
2 cup water	¼ tsp. accent powder
½ cup tomato paste	1 tbsp. sugar
1 tsp. dry thyme	¼ tsp. cayenne pepper
½ tsp. dry basil	1 tbsp. cornstarch

Put all the ingredient in a low cooker. Cover and cook on low for 1 hour. Serving the soup hot.

Fruit Salad

½ cup peach   ½ pear

½ cup pineapple   ½ cup apple

½ cup mango   ½ bananas[mash]

½ cup cherries   ½ cup orange

½ cup strawberry   ½ cup mix berry

1 cup mix nuts   ¼ cup raisins

½ cup fruit yogurt   ½ cup cream cheese

1 tbsp. basil   1 tbsp. Lemon juice

2 tbsp. sugar   1 tbsp. parsley

1 tbsp. poppy seeds   1 tsp. ginger

Mix the fruit in a large bowl. Add remaining ingredients Add in. serve

Old-Fashioned Potato Salad

4potatoes[large]

2 tbsp. oil

2 tbsp. cider vinegar

1 tbsp. sugar

1 tbsp. chives[dry]

½ cup onion

1 cup ranch dressing

2 tsp. mustard[dry]

1 tbsp. pickle relish[sweet]

1 tsp. salt

1 tsp. paprika

½ cup avocados

1 tbsp. pimentos

½ cup celery

½ cup bell pepper

2 eggs[boiled]

1 tbsp. parsley

1 tsp. cayenne pepper

Cook potatoes and eggs until tender. Peel potatoes and eggs. place large bowl. Mashed potatoes, eggs Combine all ingredients and mix-well. chill and serve.

Macaroni Salad

2 pounds macaroni

1 pounds shrimp

1 pounds crabmeat

1/3 cup ranch dressing

1/3 cup sour cream

2 eggs[boiled]

½ cup oil

1 tbsp. lemon juice

1/3 cup cream cheese

¼ cup celery

¼ cup onion

¼ cup chives

1 tbsp. garlic

1 tbsp. dill weed

1 tbsp. parsley

1 tbsp. old-bay seasons

1 tsp. black pepper

1 tsp. cayenne pepper

1 tsp. paprika

1 tbsp. ginger powder

Cook the macaroni for 10minutes making sure the Macaroni has cooled. In a bowl combine the ingredients to the macaroni. And serve

Chicken Salad

1 pounds chicken[chopped]	½ cup celery
½ cup onion	½ cup chives
2 tbsp. lemon juice	1 tsp. cayenne pepper
1 tsp. Paprika	1 tsp. Dill weed
1 tsp. salt	1 tbsp. sugar
½ cup avocados	3 tbsp. ranch dressing
3 tbsp. sour cream	1 tsp. mustard[dry]

Place the avocados in a bowl and sprinkle with lemon Juice. Add the ingredient with the avocados and serve.

Turkey Salad

¼ cup ranch dressing

1/3 cup mustard [dry]

1 cup onion powder

1 cup celery [chopped

1 package cream cheese

1 tsp. dill weed

4 cup turkey chopped]

1/3 cup pimentos

1 tsp. Sugar

1 tsp. Salt

1 tsp. pepper

1 tbsp. Parsley

1 tsp. paprika

¼ cup avocados

Combine all ingredients except avocados. Peel The avocados and remove seeds. And cut the Avocados in pieces and add to the mixture and Mix-well. Serve

Carrot Salads

4 carrot(grated)

2 cup raisins

1 cup mandarin orange

1 cup shredded cheese

1 tbsp. orange juice

1 tbsp. sour cream

2 tbsp. ranch mix

½ cup walnut

Place the carrot in a bowl. Add all ingredients and mix-well.

Broccoli Salad

4 cup broccoli	2 tbsp. cider vinegar
1 cup apple	¼ tsp. nutmeg
½ cup apple juice	1/3 cup ranch mix
¼ cup parmesan cheese	¼ tsp. salt & pepper
½ cup yogurt	2 eggs-boil
¼ tsp. dry mustard	1 tbsp. sugar

Cook the broccoli in a pot of water until tender, then drain and cool. Cut up the apples place in a bowl. Add the sauce to the apples and broccoli and mix-well. serve

Grilled Duck

6 lb. duck

½ cup butter

½ cup brown sugar

¼ cup soy sauce

½ tsp. Allspice

½ cup duck sauce

¼ cup lemon juice

¼ cup oranges juice

¼ tsp. garlic powder

¼ tsp. Onion powder

Cut the duck in half. Place on grill over hot coals and cook on each side until done. Ina small bowl add ingredients and mix well. Then brush the mixture over the duck. Serve.

Lasagna & Shrimp

1 lb. lasagna noodles	1 tbsp. old bay seasoning
1 lb. spinach	1 tsp. nutmeg
2 cup shrimp	½ cup heavy cream
½ cup alfredo sauce	½ cup cottage cheese
½ cup ricotta cheese	¼ tsp. salt & pepper
1 tbsp. garlic powder	1 tbsp. onion powder

Cook the lasagna in boiling, salt water until tender and drain. In a large skillet add the spinach and shrimp all the ingredient cook until tender. Grease baking dish and cover bottom with a thin layer of cheese sauce. Add a layer of lasagna, a layer of spinach mixture. Repeat layers until all ingredients are used. Bake at 350 degrees for 1 hour.

Lilmama Fried Chicken

8 chicken(pieces)	¼ tsp. salt
8 cup vegetable oil	¼ tsp. pepper
2 cup flour	1 tbsp. poultry seasoning
1 cup cornstarch	1 tbsp. curry powder
2 cup milk	4 eggs
1 cup beer	¼ tsp. Paprika

Heat oil in deep fry. In a large bowl add the ingredient to make the beer batter. Cut the chicken up in pieces and soak in the batter for 20 minutes. In a medium bowl mix the flour and cornstarch together. Dip the chicken in flour mixture. Fry in deep, hot oil until brown and tender for 7 minutes and drain.

Coconut Chicken

8 piece chicken

½ cup coconut milk

¼ cup garlic

¼ cup onion

½ cup coconut flaked

¼ cup bell pepper

1 cup cheddar cheese

1 can cream of chicken

2 tbsp. coconut oil

¼ tsp. allspice

1 tsp. paprika

1 tbsp. sugar

1 tsp. curry powder

¼ tsp. tarragon

1 tsp. cornstarch

¼ tsp. salt & pepper

Cook the chicken in the coconut oil until brawn. Mix all the ingredient into a large pot, cook until thick pour the mixture over chicken. Bake at 350 degrees for 20 minutes.

LilMama'S Smother Chicken

6 pieces chicken

4 tbsp. flour

2 tbsp. oil

¼ cup celery

1 tbsp. sugar

¼ cup onion

¼ cup garlic

¼ cup bell pepper

¼ cup carrot

¼ tsp. salt and pepper

Oil in a large skillet. Chicken pieces brown in the oil. Remove from skillet. Stir the flour into the skillet and vegetables and sauté. Place the chicken in skillet and Cove. Simmer 30 minutes or until chicken is tender Serving over biscuits.

Bam's Stuffed Shrimp

1 lb. shrimp	1 tbsp. parsley flake
1 cup flour	1 tbsp. celery flake
½ cup cornmeal	1 tbsp. onion minced
2 tbsp. yogurt	1 tbsp. garlic minced
1 tbsp. hot sauce	1 tsp. dry mustard
½ cup parmesan cheese	½ cup butter
½ cup beer	1 tbsp. old bay seasoning

Sauté the onion, garlic, celery, parsley and seasonings in butter in a skillet until the onion are tender. In a large bowl add ingredient and mix. Pour the onion mixture into the bowl and mix together. Stuff the shrimp firmly with the mixture. Place the shrimp tail side up, on a greased shallow baking pan and brush with butter. Bake at 400 degrees for 45 minutes.

Chicken And Dumplings

6 lb. chicken   ½ cup oil

4 cup water   1 tbsp. parsley

1 cup onion   1 tbsp. Cayenne pepper

1 cup garlic   1 tsp. poultry

1 cup celery   1 tsp. Sage

1 tsp. thyme   1 tsp. Cumin

Place the chicken pieces in a pot with water and all ingredient. Cook until tender.

Dumplings

1 cup flour   1 tsp. baking powder

½ cup milk   ¼ tsp. salt

2 eggs   2 tbsp. butter

Place flour in a large mixing bowl. Add all ingredient together and mix-well. Drop dumplings into chicken from a tbsp. and cover. Cook for 15 minutes.

CJ'S Cream Chicken

2 cup chicken	2 cup noodles
1 cup cream of chicken	1 tsp. parsley
1 cup chicken broth	1 tsp. poultry
1 cup alfredo cheese	1 tsp. sage
1 cup cream cheese	1 tsp. basil
1 tsp. red pepper	1 tsp. Cajon
1 tsp. black pepper	1 tsp. nutmeg

Boil the chicken until it's done. Boil the egg noodles drain the water off the chicken and egg noodles mix cream of chicken and chicken broth together cook till it thickens then add the chicken and noodles to broth and cream of chicken, then add season and cheese together, and let it simmer with top for 15 minutes.

Stew Chicken

4 cup chicken[chopped]

2 chicken bouillon cube

1 tsp. adobo

4 cup potatoes[chopped]

1 cup whole tomatoes

¼ cup oil

1/3 cup vinegar

2 cup sausage[chopped]

1 garlic[chopped]

1 onion[chopped]

1 chives[chopped]

1 tsp. Italian

1 tbsp. sugar

2 tsp. cornstarch

2 tsp. Worcestershire

1 tbsp. parsley

Place all ingredients in a pot and cooker and cover Cook over low heat for 45 minutes.

Chicken Enchilada

2 cup chicken cubed

1 cup cream of chicken

½ cup sour cream

1 cup rice

¼ cup onion

1 cup Cheddar cheese

¼cup garlic

10 corn tortillas

2 tbsp. chili oil

1 tbsp. chili powder

1 tsp. cumin

1 tbsp. sugar

¼ tsp. Salt

1 /4tsp. Pepper

¼cup cream cheese

In a skillet oil and add onion and garlic sauté until tender. Stir in the wet ingredients and mix well. Add chicken and cheese mix well. Pour the mixture in a bowl add all the ingredient mix together. Fill tortillas with chicken mixture, roll up. Race seam side down in greased casseroles. On top of filled tortillas sprinkle with cheese bake at 350 degree for 35 minutes.

Noodles & Shrimps

4 cup noodles

2 cup shrimps

1 tbsp. Olgbay

1 cup cream of shrimps

1 cup cream cheese

1 tbsp. Italian

Cook the noodles in boiling salted water and drain. Cook the shrimp in a separated pot and drain. In a skillet add all the mixture. And simmer for 20 minutes.

Chicken & Apple

2 cup chicken[chopped]

2 cup apple[chopped]

1 cup cream of chicken

½ cup celery

½ tsp. paprika

1 cup brown sugar

½ tsp. cayenne pepper

1 tsp. poultry

¼ cup garlic

¼ tbsp. ginger

1/3 cup lemon juice

¼ cup onion

1 tsp. sage

1 tsp. oil

1 tsp. nutmeg

1 tbsp. thyme

In a small bowl cut up the apple with lemon juice. Cook the chicken for 15 minutes, combine all the Ingredients into a large bowl mix together. Pour the mixture into a baking pan. Bake at 350 degrees For 40 minutes.

Jerk Chicken

1 lb. chicken	1 tbsp. Onion powder
1 cup vinegar	1 tbsp. garlic powder
1 tbsp. lime juice	1 tbsp. chives
2 tbsp.soy sauce	1 tbsp. Jerk seasons
1 tbsp. brown sugar	1 tbsp. thyme
½ cup oil	1 tsp. allspice
1 tsp. cloves	1 tsp. cinnamon
1 tsp. nutmeg	¼ tsp. cayenne pepper
1 tsp. ginger	¼ tsp. salt

Combine all the ingredients except the chicken. Rinse The chicken pieces well. Place the chicken in a bag pour The mixture over chicken. Chicken in the refrigerator for 24 hours. Preheat 350 degree. Bake for 30 minutes

Orange Glaze Fish

2 lb. fish

1/3 cup lemon juice

1 cup orange juice

2 tbsp. cornstarch

¼ tsp. salt

¼ tsp. pepper

1/3 cup brawn sugar

1/3 cup corn syrup

Place fish in baking dish and marinate in lemon juice mixture in refrigerator for 30 minutes. Make the glaze. Whisk the brown sugar orange juice and cornstarch In the pot cook 10 minutes. Pour the mixture over the Fish. Bake at 350 degree for 30minutes.

Old-Fashioned Pork Chops

6 pork chops

½ cup water

1 tsp. cayenne pepper

½ tsp. salt

1 tbsp. garlic

1 tbsp. onion

2 tbsp. oil

2 tbsp. vinegar

Combine all seasons on both sides pork chops. Bake at 350 degrees for 45 minutes.

Cajun Pork chops

4 pork chops	1 tsp. chili powder
2 tbsp. oil	1 tbsp. cayenne pepper
3 tbsp. rice flour	1 tbsp. paprika
1 cup beef broth	1 tsp. parsley
1 tbsp. onion powder	¼ tsp. salt & pepper
1 tbsp. garlic powder	1 tsp. allspice
1 tsp. thyme	1 tsp. ginger

Combine all the seasons into a small bowl. Pork chops with oil both sides add all the Seasons on top. Put the rice flour on the Pork chop. Bake at 350 degree 45 minute

Bake Ham

20 lb. Ham	1 tbsp. ginger powder
½ cup brown sugar	1 tbsp. cloves powder
½ cup maple syrup	1/3 cup onion powder
1 cup pineapple juice	1/3 cup garlic powder
1/3 cup celery	1 tbsp. Butter
¼ tsp. pepper	¼ tsp. Salt

Place the ham in baking pan and the mixture cook for 1 hour.

Lilmama Goulash

1 lb. shrimp	½ cup tomato
1 lb. beef	1 tbsp. parsley
1 lb. sausage	1 tsp. cayenne pepper
½ cup corn	1/3 cup onion
1 cup tomato sauce	1/3 cup garlic
1 lb. okra	½ tsp. thyme
1/3 cup celery	1 tbsp. goulash[seasoning]

Brown the beef into a skillet and onion garlic and sausage. Combine all other ingredients into the skillet. Simmer for 15minutes. serve

Bake Oxtail

4 lb. oxtail

2 cup chicken stock

½ cup onion

½ cup garlic

1 tbsp. sugar

1 tbsp. flour

1 tbsp. parsley

1 tbsp. bay leaves

¼ tsp. salt

¼ tsp. pepper

1 tbsp. hot sauce

½ cup celery

Preheat oven 350 degree combine all the season together. Put into the pot with oxtail. Bake for 30 minutes.

Jambalaya

1 lb. sausage	2 tbsp. bacon drippings
1 lb. shrimp	½ tsp. cayenne pepper
½ lb. bacon	½ tsp. hot sauce
½ cup celery chopped]	1 tsp. thyme
½ cup onion	1 tsp. allspice
½ cup garlic	1 tsp. paprika
½ cup bell pepper	1 cup tomato sauce
2 cup shrimp stock	½ cup butter
1 cup whole tomato	¼ tsp. basil
1 tsp. ginger	¼ cup parsley

In a large skillet brown the bacon add sausage and cook stirring occasionally, add the ingredient cook until tender. Cut each shrimp into thirds cook until shrimp begins to turn pink add the shrimp to the mixture cook for 20 minutes let jambalaya develop for 10 minutes before serving.

Old-fashioned pork chops

6 pork chops

1 tsp. Cajon Seasons

1 tbsp. cayenne Pepper

½ cup water

1 tbsp. garlic

1 tbsp. onion

2 tbsp.oil

Combine all seasons on both sides Pork chops. Bake at 350 degrees for 45 minutes.

Roast Turkey

1 10 lb. turkey   ½ tsp. salt

1 butter[sticks]   ½ tsp. pepper

½ cup water

1. Rinse turkey with running cold water, drain well

2. Place the turkey with its breast side up, on a rack in a large open roasting pan. Brush the skin lightly with butter to keep the turkey moist and allow the skin to color evenly. Bake at 375 degrees. Roast for 30 minutes.

Carolyn Jean Franklin Allen

Beef Loaf

1 lb. ground beef

½ cup cream

½ cup cheese

1 egg

1 cup. bread crumbs

1 tbsp. Worcestershire

½ cup tomato sauce

1 tbsp. Parsley

1 tbsp. Thyme

1 tsp. Onion powder

1 tsp. garlic powder

½tsp. Mustard [dry]

½tsp.salt

½ tsp. Pepper

Combine all ingredients and blend well, place In a loaf pan. Bake at 375 degrees for 1 hour

Bake Chicken

5 lb. chicken   ½ cup margarine

1 cup chicken stock   1 tsp. Salt and pepper

Cut the chicken in small pieces and place in A bake pan. Cook the chicken in stock. Add The margarine salt and pepper. Bake at 350 Degrees for 25 minute.

Avocados & Mango Pancake

1 cup avocados

1 cup mango

2 cup flour

2 eggs

½ cup milk

1 tbsp. baking powder

2 tbsp. sugar

¼ tsp. salt

1 tbsp. lemon juice

2 tbsp. butter

Into a large bowl combine the mango, avocados, lemon juice and sugar and mash. Add all dry ingredient together. Combine all the mixture together. Drop by spoonfuls onto a hot, greased pancake griddle and cook until bubbles turn and brown on other side.

Lilmama Doughnuts

2 cup flour

1 cup sugar

2 tbsp. yeast

½ cup butter

2 eggs

¼ cup milk

¼tsp. Nutmeg

¼ tsp. Mace

¼ tsp. salt

¼cup water

¼ tsp. cinnamon

¼ tsp. allspice

Dissolve the yeast in warm water. Combine all the ingredients in a large bowl. Mix until smooth. Chill over night. Drop by tsp. into hot deep fry for 3 minutes or brown. Drain on absorbent paper.

Strawberry Shortbread

2 cup flour

½ cup sugar

¼ cup heavy cream

2 eggs

1 tbsp. baking powder

1 tsp. strawberry extract

¼ tsp. cake spice

¼ tsp. salt

Strawberry Syrup

2 cup strawberry mashed   1/3 cup powder sugar

¼ tsp. strawberry extract

In a large bowl add the wet ingredients. Pour dry into the wet mix until dough is moist and forms a ball. Drop by spoonfuls onto ungreased sheet. Into a bowl add the strawberry and mash then up. Add the sugar, extract mix together, Bake at 400 degree for 15 minutes. Remove from the oven, let cool. Split into two layers, spread the strawberry mixture between the layers. serve

Banana At Chocolate Waffle

2 cup flour

½ cup sugar

½ cup milk

½ cup coca powder

1 tsp. rum[extract]

1/3 tsp. salt

1 cup banana [mashed]

2 eggs

¼ cup butter

3 tsp. baking powder

1 tsp. cinnamon

¼ tsp. vanilla [extract]

Sift dry ingredients together into a bow! add the Wet ingredients into the dry mixture. Mash the banana In the small bowl, then add to the mixture and mix-well, Cooking a hot waffle iron until brown.

Almond Joy Brownies

½ cup wheat flour

½ cup flour

½ cup brown sugar

½ cup sugar

½ cup chocolate chips

1 tsp. almond extract

1 cup almond

1 tbsp. baking powder

½ cup butter

½ cup cocoa powder

3 eggs

¼ tsp. salt

½ tsp. cocoa powder

1 cup coconut

Sift the dry ingredients together into a large bowl. Into a small bowl whisk together all the wet ingredient. Pour the wet ingredient into the dry ingredient and mix well. Pour ½ mixture into the baking pan. Pour some coconut and almond on top the mixture- The remaining mixture On top. Preheat the oven to 350 degrees. Grease the Baking for 30 minutes, cool.

Rodell Waffles

2 cup flour

1 tbsp. Baking powder

1 tbsp. sugar

2 eggs

¼ cup oi1

1 cup chocolate chip

2 bananas [mashed]

1 tsp. vanilla extract

1 ¼ cup milk

Combine the ingredient into a large bowl mix well Preheat a waffles iron. Pour the mixture into the waffles iron. Cook until brown.

Naeva's Jalapeno Cornbread

1 cup flour

1 cup cornmeal

½ cup sugar

2 cup jalapeno(chopped)

1 cup bacon(chopped)

1 cup cheese(grated)

1 tbsp. baking powder

¼ tsp. salt

¼ tsp. nutmeg

½ cup butter

½ cup heavy cream

3 eggs

Mix the dry ingredient in a large bowl. Mix the wet ingredient in a small bowl. Pour the wet into the dry and mix well. Stir in the jalapeno and cheese and bacon and mix. Melt the butter in a large iron skillet and pour the cornbread mixture into the skillet. Bake at 350 degrees for 40 minutes or until done.

Fig Shortbread

2 cup flour

½ cup brown sugar

½ cup sugar

1 cup figs

½ cup almond

3 eggs

1 tbsp. baking powder

¼ tsp. ground cloves

½ tsp. almond extract

½ cup butter

½ cup heavy cream

¼ tsp. Salt

In a large bowl add dry ingredients mix. In a small bowl add wet ingredients mix. Pour the wet into dry and mix together. Grease a glass casserole. Pour the mixture into casserole bake at 350 degrees for minutes.

Ginger Bread

2 cup flour

½ cup butter

1 cup brown sugar

½ cup sour cream

½ cup molasses

4 eggs

¼ tsp. Salt

½ cup ginger paste

1 tbsp. baking powder

1 tsp. cinnamon

1 tsp. allspice

½ tsp. cloves

1 tsp. honey

1 tsp. ginger powder

Preheat the oven to 375 degrees. Butter and Hour the baking pan. In a large bowl, combine all the wet ingredient and mix-well. Add dry ingredients alternately with the cream mixture. Pour the mixture into baking pan. Bake for 45 minutes.

Lilmama Bread Pudding

12 biscuits

2 cup buttermilk

4 eggs

2 cup sugar

1 tsp. vanilla extract

¼ tsp. nutmeg

¼ tsp. cinnamon

½ cup butter

In a large bowl soak 12 biscuits in buttermilk over night. Add the ingredient to the mixture. Grease baking dish. Baking dish. Bake at 350 degrees for 30 minutes.

Regina Bread Pudding

4 cup bread crumbs	1/3 cup yeast
½ cup raisins	¼ tsp. cardamom
½ cup brown sugar	¼ tsp. poppy seeds
½ cup chocolate liqueur	¼ tsp. Salt
1/3 cup almond butter	¼ tsp. cinnamon
½ cup almond	1 tbsp. almond extract
½ cup butter	¼ tsp. lemon juice
1 cup cream cheese	1/3 cup milk
2 cup apples	1 cup heavy cream
1 cup chocolate chips	3 eggs

Preheat oven 350degree. Grease a baking dish. Combine the wet ingredients in a large bowl. Dissolve the yeast in the milk in a bowl Add all the dry ingredients to the mix stir until smooth. Let rise for 20 minutes. Pour the mixture baking dish. Bake for 30 minutes. Remove from the oven and let cool before serving.

Lilmama Buttermilk Biscuits

2 cup flour

1 cup buttermilk

¼ cup shortening

1 tbsp. baking powder

¼ tsp. salt

¼ tsp. nutmeg

Sift dry ingredients together twice and place in a bowl. Add in the shortening until well mixed. Add the buttermilk and stir well. Drop by tablespoons onto greased baking sheet. Bake at 400 degrees for 10 minutes.

Hot Water Cornbread

1 cup cornmeal

1 cup flour

½ cup dry milk

1 cup hot water

1 egg

¼ tsp. Salt

1 tbsp oil

1 tbsp. baking powder

1 tbsp. baking soda

2 tbsp. sugar

Preheat a skillet over medium heat. Into a pot boil water in a large bowl. Add the dry ingredients. Add the egg, hot water. Into the skillet 1 cup oil drop the cornbread mixture into the skillet. Fry 3 or until brown drain on paper towels.

Buttermilk Cornbread

1 cup cornmeal   ½ stick butter

1 cup flour   1 tbsp. baking powder

½ cup sugar   ¼ tsp. salt

1 cup buttermilk   2 eggs

Preheat the oven to 400 degrees. Grease baking pan. Combine the dry ingredient together. Add the wet ingredients into the mix-well, pour the mixture into the Baking pan. Bake for 30 minutes.

Cranberry Bread

½ cup cornmeal

2 cup flour

1 cup sugar

½ cup butter

½ cup cream cheese

1/3 cup cream

2 eggs

1 cup cranberry sauce

1 tbsp. orange zest

1 tbsp. baking powder

¼ tsp. salt

1 tsp. cardamom

1 tsp. mace

1 tsp. allspice

½ cup raisins

½ cup cranberry juice

Combine the cranberry sauce, cranberry juice in a pot and cook over low heat, for 5minutes. Cool, into a large bowl cream the wet ingredient together sift the flour with the dry ingredient. Add to creamed mixture alternately with cranberry mixture then add the flour mixture blending well. Pour into greased pan. Bake at 350 degrees for 45 minutes.

Lilmama Biscuits

2 cup flour	1 tbsp. sugar
1 tbsp. baking powder	1 tsp. salt
1 cup milk	½ butter
1 cup cheese	1 tbsp. honey

Sift dry ingredients together twice and place in a bowl. Cut in the butter until well mixed. Add the milk and stir Well. Bake at 400 degrees for 10 minutes.

Bananas Nut Corn Bread

1 cup bananas[crushed]   ½ cup nuts

1 cup cornmeal   ½ cup sugar

1 tbsp. baking powder   2 eggs

1 cup flour   ½ cup milk

¼ cup oil   ½ tsp. Salt

Combine the dry ingredients in a large bowl. Combine the wet ingredients in a small bowl. Mix-well the ingredients. Oil the pan and pour The mixture into the pan. Bake 425 degrees For 20 minutes.

Carolyn Jean Franklin Allen

Old-Fashioned Corn Bread

I cup cornmeal

1 cup flour

½ cup sugar

3 tbsp. oil

1 tsp. salt

1 tbsp. baking powder

½ cup milk

2 eggs

Sift dry ingredients together into a bowl. Add the Wet ingredients into a small bowl. Add all the ingredients together mix well. Grease the pan With oil. Pour into pan. Bake for 30 minutes.

Cheese Corn Bread

1 cup flour	2 eggs
1 cup corn meal	1 cup milk
½ cup sugar	1 tsp. baking powder
1 cup cheese[shredded]	1 tsp. salt

Add the eggs, milk, cheese into a large bowl. Stir In dry ingredients blender together. Greased the Pan. Pour into pan. Bake for 20 minutes,

Banana nut Bread

2 cup flour

1 cup sugar

¼ cup butter melt] 2eggs

1 cup banana crushed)

¼ cup nut

Cream the butter, sugar, eggs, bananas into a large Bowl. Add the flour, nuts until well mixed. Pour into A greased loaf pan. Bake in 350 degrses over for 1 hour

CJ"S Oat Muffins

2 cup oat flour	1 tbsp. baking powder
1 cup oatmeal	½ tsp. baking soda
1 cup brown sugar	½ tsp. vanilla powder
½ cup butter	½ tsp. almond powder
½ cup almond butter	½ tsp. poppy seeds
½ cup soy milk	½ tsp. cake spice
3 eggs	½ cup almond
1 cup raisins	1/3 cup molasses

Preheat oven 350 degrees. Mix the wet ingredients in a bowl. Into a large bowl mix the dry ingredients. Combine all the ingredients together. Mix-well, pour the oat mixture into greased muffin tins. Bake for 20 minutes.

Snowball Cookies

2 cup flour

½ cup powder sugar

1 cup butter

2 cup mix nuts

1 tsp. vanilla extract

1 tsp. Almond extract

1 cup sugar

½ cup coconuts(shredded)

Cream butter and sugar, then add the ingredients except powder sugar roll into a balls and place on a baking sheet. Bake at 350 degrees for 15 minutes. While still hot, shake in bag of powder sugar. Servings.

Lilmama Oatmeal Cookies

1 cup flour

1 ½ cup brown sugar

2 ¼ cup oatmeal

1/3 cut maple syrup

2 eggs

½ tsp. salt

2 tsp. vanilla extract

1 tsp. baking soda

1 tsp. baking powder

½ cup butter

Sift the dry ingredient together. Add all at once to the Flour mixture and mix well. Drop by spoonful onto greased cookie sheet. Bake at 375 degrees for 15 minutes.

Sugar Cookies

2 cup flour

½ cup sugar

½ cup brown sugar

½ cup cream[heavy]

2 eggs

1 tbsp. baking powder

¼ tsp. salt

1 tsp. cinnamon

1 tsp. almond extract

1 cup nuts[almond]

Mix the wet ingredients together Fold in remaining ingredients and drop by tbsp. onto greased cookie Sheet. Bake at 325 degrees for about 20 minutes.

Corny Dogs Muffins

12 hot dogs [chopped]   1 tsp. salt

1 cup cornmeal   2 eggs

1 cup flour   ½ cup milk

½ cup sugar   ¼ cup oil

1 tbsp. baking powder   1 tbsp. dry mustard

Heat oven to 400 degrees, Grease twelve muffin pan. Combine all the ingredients in a large bowl. Cut up Twelve hot dogs. Put the hot dogs in the mixture. Fill muffin cups ½ fill. bake at 400 degrees for 15 minutes or until browned.

Peanut Butter & Banana

1 cup wheat flour

1 tsp. baking powder

1 tsp. baking soda

½ tsp. salt

½ cup sugar

½ cup brown sugar

½ cup peanut butter

1 cup banana[mash]

½ cup butter

¼ cup almonds

1 tsp. vanilla[extract]

2 eggs

In a large mix bowl combine all the ingredients together and mix-well. Heat the over to 350 degrees Bake for 10 or 15 minutes or until brown.

Banana Muffins

2 cup wheat flour

1 cup brown sugar

½ cup coca powder

1 cup yogurt

1 tsp. baking powder

1 cup banana [mashed]

1 tbsp. ginger

¼ cup butter

2 eggs

Sift dry ingredients together into a bowl. In a small bowl the wet ingredients. Pour the wet into the dry And mix well. Add the banana and stir until blended Greased muffin pan ½ full. Bake in 400 degree oven For 20 minutes.

Strawberry Muffin

2 cup strawberries

2 cup flour

1 cup sugar

2 eggs

1 tsp. salt

1 cup cream cheese

½ cup butter

1 cup sour cream

1 tbsp. baking powder

1 tbsp. strawberry [extract]

Sift the dry ingredients together. Mix the wet ingredients, cut the strawberry up into a bowl a put with the mixture. Pour the wet into the dry ingredients mix well together. Pour the mixture into the muffin pan. Bake at 350 degrees for 30 minutes.

Romance Cookies

2 cup flour

½ cup sugar

½ cup brown sugar

1 tsp. liqueur

1 tsp. alspice

2 eggs

½ cup butter

1 tbsp. baking powder

1 tsp. vanilla extract

1 tsp. salt

Combine all the ingredient into a bowl. mix-well Drop from a teaspoon onto ungreased cookie sheet Bake for 15 minutes at 350 degrees,

Peach Cobbler

4 cup peach [sliced]

3 cup peach juice

½ cup butter

¼ cup baking mix

Pastry

2 cup baking mix

½ cup milk

½ tsp. nutmeg

½ tsp. cinnamon

¼ tsp. allspice

½ cup brown sugar

1 cup brown sugar

½ cup butter

In a bowl combine all the ingredient for the pastry and Mix form into ball. Into a baking pan pour the peach mixture. Onto the top pour the pastry mixture, Bake At 350 degree for 40 minutes or until brown.

Velvet Rose Cupcake

2 cup flour

1 cup sugar

½ cup brown sugar

½ cup butter

½ cup peanut butter

3 eggs

1/3 cup sour cream

½ cup walnut

1 tbsp. baking powder

¼ tsp. salt

1 tsp. vanilla extract

½ cup cocoa powder

1 tsp. vinegar

1 tsp. cake spice

10 drops of red food coloring

In a small bowl combine the wet ingredient together In a large bowl add the dry ingredient together. Pour the wet into the dry and mix together. Grease and flour muffin cups. Pour the mixture into the muffin cups. Bake at 350 degrees for 20 minutes.

Peppermint Patties

2 ½ cup flour	2 tbsp. baking powder
1 cup sugar	¼ tsp. salt
1 cup butter	¼ tsp. peppermint extract
2 eggs	1 tsp. Almond extract
1 cup almond	1 cup peppermint candy

Into a large bowl crush up peppermint and almond together. Into a bowl cream the sugar and butter together Blend in the eggs and extracts. Sift all the dry ingredient together. Add the dry with the wet blend well. Stir in the almond and peppermint. Roll out to ¼-inch round cutter. Place on greased cook sheets, Preheat oven to 350 degrees. Bake for 10 minutes, then cool.

Cream Cheese Peppermint

1 cup cream cheese

2 tbsp. butter

1 cup powder sugar

1 tsp. Peppermint extract

Combine ingredients mix until smooth, dip cookies, place on waxed paper and let stand until set.

Spaghetti & Meatballs

1 lb. ground lamb

½ cup oatmeal

¼ cup heavy cream

1/3 cup cream cheese

¼ cup butter

1 eggs

1 lb. spaghetti

¼ tsp. garlic powder

¼ tsp. onion powder

¼ tsp. marjoram

1 tbsp. Brown sugar

¼ tsp. parsley

¼ tsp. Dry mustard

2 cup tomatoes

Meat ball: in a large bowl add the lamb and all the ingredient mix-well. Roll into a medium ball. Brown in batches in a skillet. Cook the spaghetti in boiling, salt water until tender and drain. Add the tomatoes sauce and meat balls to the spaghetti. Serve

Lilmama Grits-Gravy

2 cup gritys

3 cup water

1 cup shredded cheese

½ cup milk

½ cup heavy cream

1/3 cup flour

½ cup butter

¼ tsp. accent powder

1 tbsp. Sugar

¼ cup minced onion

¼ cup minced garlic

¼ tsp. pepper

1 tbsp. Worcestershire sauce

Stir grits and salt into boiling water. Cook until thick. Add all the ingredient into pot. Into a medium pot, add the flour and stir in the ingredients to make gravy. Bring to boil until gravy is thick and bubbly.

Bonnie's Candy Apples

6 med. apples

½ cup water

1 cup sugar

1 cup corn syrup

¼ tsp. peppermint extract

¼ tsp. cinnamon

2 tbsp. red food coloring

1/3 cup hard red candies

Wash and dry the apples and insert a wooden stick into stem end of each apple. Mix ingredients in a pot and cook to hard-crack stage. Dip apples into mixture quickly and place on greased waxed paper. Cool.

CJ'S Popcorn Balls

2 cup popcorn

1 cup hazelnut spread

2 cup hazelnut

1 cup raisins

1 cup milk

1 cup corn syrup

½ cup brown sugar

1 tbsp. vinegar

½ cup butter

1 tsp. vanilla extract

1 tsp. Cinnamon

¼ tsp. nutmeg

Heat the oil in corn popper Add the popcorn and cove until popping stops. Over medium heat and cook until mixture reaches 260 degrees. Carefully pour the mixture over popcorn. Let sit for 2 minutes. With well-oiled hands, form balls. Place on oiled waxed paper and cool completely.

Peanut Butter Apples

6 med. apple

½ cup peanut butter

1 cup sugar

½ cup butter

½ tsp. honey

½ tsp. maple flavor

½ cup com syrup

½ cup heavy cream

Wash and dry the apple and insert a wooden stick into stem end of each apple. Combine ingredients in a pot and cook, stirring to 230 degrees on candy thermometer. Dip each apple into mixture and swirl until well coated. Place on greased waxed paper. Cool.

CJ'S Ice Cream Sandwiches

12 peanut butter cookies

2 cup banana(mash)

1 cup hazelnut spread

8 cup ice cream

Into a large bowl mash banana and add the Ice cream mix-well. On a cookie sheet lay the cookies out. Spread the hazelnut spread over the top. Chill for 1 hour. Put the ice cream on top of the cookies. Chill for 1 hour. Serve.

Apricot Cobbler

2 cup apricot   ¼ tsp. lemon juice

3 cup orange juice   ¼ tsp. cornstarch

1 cup sugar   ¼ tsp. cinnamon

2 cup apple   ½ cup butter

Dumplings

2 cup baking mix   2/3 cup milk

1 cup sugar   ¼ tsp. cinnamon

Into a bowl stir all ingredient until soft dough forms. Drop by spoonfuls onto the cobbler, pour the mixture into baking dish. Bake at 350 degrees for 45 minutes.

Chocolate Banana Pudding

10 ripe banana

2 cup heavy cream

2 egg yolks

2/3 cup cocoa powder

1 cup brown sugar

4cup chocolate graham Cracker crumbs

3 tbsp. butter

½ tsp. cinnamon

½ tsp. nutmeg

½ tsp. poppy seeds

3 tbsp. cornstarch

1 tsp. Espresso powder

¼ tsp. Salt

1 tsp. banana extract

Combine sugar, cornstarch, salt and cream, spice in a large sauce pan. Cook and stir on medium heat until thickened. Add a little hot mixture to eggs and blend well. Pour eggs into mixture in sauce pan. Add butter and blend mixture well. Cover pudding. Cool slightly. Spread a small amount of the graham cracker crumbs on the bottom of the dish, Top with a layer of sliced banana. Spoon the pudding over bananas. Continue layering graham cracker, banana, and pudding to make three layers. Cove and chill until serve.

Noodle Pudding

2 cup noodle crumbs   ¼ tsp. Pie spice

1 cup sugar   1 tsp. vanilla extract

1 cup heavy cream   ½ cup cream cheese

1 cup black berry   1 tbsp. Liqueur(berry)

Blend the noodle in a food processor until the noodle is crumbs. Then put in a pot with ingredients bring to a boil and mix well. Except the blackberry. Pour the blackberry on top and mix. serve

Pumpkin Pudding

1 cup pumpkin(mashed)

½ cup marshmallows

1 cup flour

½ cup brown sugar

¼ cup sugar

½ cup butter

1 tbsp. baking powder

1 tbsp. pumpkin spice

½ cup buttermilk

3 eggs

¼ tsp. salt

1 tsp. vanilla extract

Cream the wet ingredient together. In a bowl combine all dry ingredients Together. Pour the wet into the dry mix well. Pour mixture into baking pan. Bake at 350 degrees for 1 hour

Turkey Sandwiches

8 slices turkey

4 slices wheat bread

4 slice Cheddar cheese

4 slice turkey bacon

4 slice lettuce

½ cup cj sauce

4 slices tomatoes

4 slices pickles

6 slice avocado

6 dice jalapeno pepper

In a small bowl add ¼ cup yogurt, ¼ cup yellow mustard, ¼ cup cream cheese, 1 tbsp. Honey, 1 tbsp. hot sauce, 1 tsp. lemon juice, ¼ tsp. onion powder, ¼ tsp. Garlic powder, 1 tsp. vinegar, 1 tbsp. chili oil, 2 tbsp. ketchup, mix well. Spread sauce on side of each bread slice. Add the turkey, and all the ingredients. And serve the sandwiches.

Mama's Peach And Cream Oatmeal

2 cup oatmeal   ½ cup butter

1 cup peach(sliced)   ½ cup brown sugar

1 cup heavy cream   ¼ tsp. Cinnamon

2 cup water   1 tbsp. honey

Bring water to a boil in a pot Whisk in the oatmeal, once the oatmeal is mixed. Add the remaining ingredients in the pot, and mix well. Cove and simmer for 15 minutes.

Shakira Fruit Rolls

2 can cinnamon roll

½ cup cream cheese

2 cup strawberry

2 cup banana

1 tbsp. sugar

2 cup mango

2 cup peaches

2 cup blackberry

1 tbsp. vanilla extract

1 lemon juice

Prepare roll the dough out according to package directions. Cream cheese room temperature. Squeaky the lemon juice Over the banana. Combine the blackberry, strawberry, peaches, mango in a bowl. Let rise for about 1 hour. Place On a greased baking sheet. Bake at 375 degrees for 20 Minutes or until done. Then cool. Mix the sugar, vanilla, lemon juice until smooth and spread on the cinnamon roll.

Tia Cream Bar

¼ cup brown sugar

1 ½ cup graham cracker

1 cup cream cheese

1 cup cream

1 tsp. cinnamon

½ tsp. Nutmeg

½ tsp. ginger

1 cup pecans

Combine the brown sugar graham cracker, spices into a large bowl mix well Add the cream cheese and cream pour into baking pan and chill for 30 minutes.

Deviled Eggs

6 eggs

1 tbsp. dry mustard

2 tbsp. Pickle relish

½ tbsp. ranch dressing

1 tbsp. Honey

1 tbsp. paprika

A large pot gently add the eggs and water to boil Cook 15 minutes over medium heat. Remove the Eggs from the water and cool. Peel the eggs and Cut them in half. Remove the yolks to a small bowl And place the whites eggs on a plate. Crush the yolk with A fork and add all ingredients mix well. Spoonful of the yolk Mixture into each egg white half. Sprinkle with paprika and Serve.

Barbecued Beans

1 lb. ground beef	¼ tsp. salt
½ cup onion(chopped)	¼ tsp. pepper
½ cup garlic(chopped)	¼ tsp. hot sauce
2 cup pinto beans	1/3 cup liquid smoke
¼ cup molasses	¼ tsp. chili oil
1 cup brown sugar	¼ tsp. cardamom powder
½ cup butter	2 tbsp. vinegar
1/3 cup honey	¼ tsp. hot sauce
1/3 cup catsup	1 cup pineapple crushed

Brown the ground beef and onion and garlic and pour off the fat. Add remaining ingredients and mix well, then pour into a casserole. Bake at 350 degrees for 30 minutes.

Barbecued Stuffed Potatoes

6 lge. baking potatoes

1 lb. ground beef

¼ cup barbecue sauce

½ cup butter

½ cup sour cream

¼ tsp. Oregano

2 cup grated cheese

¼tsp. Chives

¼ tsp. garlic powder

¼ tsp Parsley

¼ tsp. salt

¼ tsp. pepper

½ tsp. cumin

¼ tsp. Paprika

Brown the ground beef and pour off the fat. Wash the potatoes and wipe dry. Bake in a 400 degrees oven for 1 hr. or until done. Cut a slice from top of each potato. Scoop out potatoes leaving shells intact. Place the potatoes in a bowl and add all ingredient and mix well. Bake at 350 degrees for 20 minutes.

Mama's Rice Pudding

2 cup rice	1 tsp. nutmeg
3 cup water	1 tsp. cinnamon
1 cup sugar	½ cup raisin
2 cup milk	¼ tsp. Salt
1 cup peach	½ cup butter
2 eggs	2 tsp. vanilla extract

Cook the rice in salt water for 20 minutes. In a large bowl mix all ingredients and pour the mixture into a casserole. Bake at 350 degrees for one hour.

Liver & Rice

1 lb. liver	1 tbsp. minced garlic
1 cup rice	1 tsp. turmeric
1 cup brown gravy	¼ tsp. sage
¼ cup milk	1 tbsp. minced onion
1/3 cup chili oil	1 tsp. Marjoram
1 tbsp. Parsley	¼ tsp. salt & pepper

Cook the rice until lightly browned. Cook the liver until tender. Add all the ingredient into a mix bowl and mix well. Pour the mixture in a grease baking dish. Bake at 350 degrees for 30 minutes.

Lamb & Rice

2 lb. ground lamb

2 cup rice

1 cup pineapple

1 cup evaporated milk

½ cup diced tomatoes

¼ cup chili oil

1 cup cheddar cheese

1 tbsp. sugar

1 tsp. onion powder

1 tsp. garlic powder

1 tbsp. curry powder

1 tbsp. rosemary

¼ tsp. Salt & pepper

1 tbsp. Celery

Cook the rice for 10 minutes. In a large skillet brown the lamb. into a large mix bowl add all the ingredient mix well. Pour the mixture into a casseroles. Bake at 350 for 15 minutes.

Scallop Potato

8 cup potato(sliced)

2 cup shredded cheese

½ cup sour cream

1 cup turkey bacon

½ cup butter

½ cup heavy cream

¼ tsp. allspice

¼ cup minced onion

¼ cup minced garlic

1 tbsp. lemon juice

1 tbsp. parsley

¼ tsp. salt

¼ tsp. pepper

2 tbsp. cornstarch

In a large bowl mix all ingredient together. Set the potato on the aside. Place potato in a casserole then cove with the cheese mixture repeat layering bake at 350 degree for 30 minutes.

BRUSSELS SPROUTS

2 cup Brussels sprouts

1 cup cheese

½ cup bread crumbs

1 cup bacon

½ cup sour cream

¼ cup onion

½ cup pine nuts

¼ tsp. salt & pepper

¼ tsp. nutmeg

¼ tsp. sugar

2 tbsp. vinegar

2 tbsp. cornstarch

¼ cup garlic

1/3 cup bacon grease

Cook the bacon in a large skillet over medium heat. When browned and crisp, add the Brussels sprouts cook until tender, add all the ingredients and cook for 20 minutes,4-6 servings.

Stuffed Tomato

4 large tomatoes

2 cup spinach

½ cup turkey bacon

1 cup cream cheese

¼ cup canola oil

½ cup heavy cream

¼ cup minced onion

¼ cup minced garlic

¼ tsp. Nutmeg

¼ tsp. salt & pepper

Into a large skillet. Add spinach and all ingredient and cook for 10 minutes. Cut the tomatoes and remove the ribs, and seeds. stuff the tomatoes with the spinach mixture. Bake at 350 degrees for 30 minutes.

Creole Carrot

2 cup diced chicken	½ cup chicken broth
2 cup carrot	¼ tsp. dry mustard
2 cup banana	1 tsp. curry powder
1 cup cheese	1 tbsp. lemon juice
½ cup raisins	1 tbsp. honey
2 tbsp. minced onion	1 tbsp. Creole powder
2 tbsp. minced garlic	¼ tsp. nutmeg
½ cup almond	¼ tsp. almond butter
½ cup butter	½ cup brown sugar
1 cup milk	1 tsp. parsley

Preheat oven to 350 degrees. Wash and cut into 1-inch pieces. Cook, covered, in boiling, salted water for 15 minutes or until tender. Into a large bowl mash banana. Combine all the ingredient together mix-well. Pour the mixture into casserole. Bake for 40 minutes.

Mama's lima bean

2 cup lima bean

1 cup bacon(diced)

4 cup water

1 tsp. onion powder

4 tbsp. bacon fat

¼ tsp. accent powder

¼ tsp. pepper

1 tsp. Garlic powder

Place the bean and water in a pot and bring to a boil. Cook for 20 minutes. In a large skillet brown the bacon and save the bacon fat. Pour the beans into the skillet with the bacon and the ingredients and simmer 10 minutes. Serve.

Cabbage With Cheese Sauce

1 large cabbage

1 large eggplant

½ cup bacon(diced)

¼ cup walnuts

1cup heavy cream

1 cup shredded Swiss cheese

½ cup cream cheese

¼ tsp. cayenne pepper

1 tbsp. celery flake

1 tbsp. parsley flaked

¼ cup bacon fat

1/3 cup sour cream

1 tbsp. flour

¼ tsp. nutmeg

1 tbsp. sugar

1 tbsp. Vinegar

Cut cabbage and eggplant into pieces. Cook in salt boiling water until tender, 10 or 15 minutes, drain well. In skillet brown bacon remove from heat. Stir in flour and cream cook until mixture boils and thickens, stirring constantly. Add remaining ingredients, stir until cheese is melted. Add cabbage and eggplant and bacon simmer 15 minutes. Servings.

EGGPLANT MOZZARELLA CHEESE

½ cup onion

1 cup bread crumbs

1 eggplant

1 tbsp. olive oil

1cup mozzarella cheese

¼ tsp. Salt

¼ tsp. Black pepper

½ tsp. garlic

2 tbsp. parmesan cheese

Cut the eggplants into 1-inch thick slices, Place the eggplant in casserole. Into large bowl combine the ingredients mix-well. Pour the mixture oven the eggplant, add the cheese. Bake at 325 degrees for 30 minutes or until tender.

Broccoli And Mango

2 cup couscous	½ tsp. thyme
2 cup broccoli	¼ tsp. nutmeg
2 cup mango	¼ tsp. brown sugar
½ cup mango juice	2 tsp. olive oil
1 cup cheese	¼ tsp. onion powder
½ cup almond	¼ tsp. garlic powder
2 tsp. sesame oil	¼ tsp. salt & pepper

Into a range pot add the juice with broccoli cook for 3 minute. Add the seasoning and mango and cheese And cook until tender. In a pot with boil water stir in The couscous, remove from the gently separate the couscous and fluff them up. Combine the couscous with broccoli mixture and serve.

Cream Corn

4 cup corn

2 cup cream[heavy]

1 cup cream cheese

¼ cup sugar

¼ tsp. Cornstarch

½ cup butter

1 tsp. Onion powder

1 tsp. Garlic powder

¼ tsp. Paprika

¼ tsp. Salt & pepper

In a large skillet over medium heat, melt butter. Add corn And seasonings. Cook for 10 minutes add cream cheese And cream lower heat, stir, cover and cook for 10 minutes.

Stuffed Bell Pepper

1 lb. ground beef

¼ cup bread crumbs

¼ cup parmesan cheese

1/3 cup tomato paste

2 tbsp. chili oil

1 egg

4 bell pepper

¼ cup onion

¼ cup garlic

1/3 cup celery

1 tbsp. ketchup

1 tsp. chili powder

¼ tsp. salt

¼ cup Worcestershire sauce

In a large bowl add all ingredient mix well. Fill pepper halves with meat mixture place in greased pan. Bake at 350 degree for 30 minutes or until top are browned.

Dirty Rice

1 beef stock[can]

1 tbsp. brown sugar

1 lb. livers[chopped]

1 lb. giblets[chopped]

1 lb. beef[ground]

1 lb. sausage[ground]

½ cup onion[green]

1 tbsp. kitchen bouquet

½ tsp. salt

½ tsp. black pepper

1 tbsp. parsley

1 tbsp. cilantro

2 tbsp. garlic[minced]

½ cup celery[chopped]

2 cup rice

1 tbsp. sauce soja

Cook the ground beef, live, giblets sausage in a large Skillet with oil until tender. Cook the rice and stir into Kitchen bouquet and sauce soja, stir in con stock. Add all ingredients in the bowl. serve

Coconut Rice

1 cup water

2 cup rice

2 cup coconut

1 tbsp. coconut oil

1 tsp. salt

1 tsp. coconut[extract]

2 cup coconut milk

1 cup sugar

In a pot water with coconut oil add the rice, cook For 10 minutes. Combine all the ingredients mix Together. Serve.

Mom's Stuffed Cabbage

1 lb. beef[ground]

1 lb. cabbage

½ cup bread crumbs

½ cup cheese

¼ cup brown sugar

½ cup tomatoes

1 tbsp. onion powder

1 tbsp. garlic powder

1 tbsp. parsley

1 tbsp. Thyme

1 eggs

1 tbsp. cayenne pepper

In a large bowl put all ingredient and mix well remove center vein of cabbage leaves. Keeping each leaf In one Piece. Immerse leaves in boiling water till limp about 3 minutes drain. Place meat mixture on each large leaf. Fold in sides roll up each leaf making sure folded sides Are included in roll. Preheat 350degrees. Bake for 1 hours.

Candy Sweet Potatoes

4 lb. sweet potatoes	1 tsp. cinnamon
½ cup brown sugar	1 tsp. nutmeg
½ cup sugar	1 tsp. ginger
1 cup marshmallows	1 tsp. mace
2 tbsp. honey	1 tsp. clove
½ butter	1 tbsp. vanilla extract
1 tbsp. molasses	1 tbsp. maple syrup

Boil sweet potatoes and ½ cook. Place into bake pan With butter. Into a pot add all ingredient cook for 15 Minutes. Pour the mixture on top for sweet potatoes. Bake at 350 degree for 30 minutes.

Cream Spinach

4 lb. spinach

1 cup avocado

1 cup bacon

½ cup cream

½ cup sour cream

½ cup sugar

1 cup cream cheese

2 tbsp. cornstarch

½ cup onion

½ cup garlic

½ cup chives

¼ tsp. cardamom

¼ tsp. salt

¼ tsp. pepper

1 tbsp. nutmeg

1 tbsp. bacon dripping

Into a large skillet place the bacon and cook until brown. Add all the ingredients and cook over low heat. For 30 minutes. Cut avocados into bite size and add to the mixture.

Chili beans

1 lb. ground beef	1 tbsp. Oil
1 lb. pinto bean	1 tsp. chili powder
1 onion[chopped]	1 tsp. thyme
1 tsp. cardamom	1 tsp. parsley
1 garlic[chopped]	1 bell pepper chopped]
1 tsp. red pepper	1 tsp. oregano
1 tomato sauce[can]	1 tomato paste can]
1 tsp. cilantro	2 tbsp. pinto bean
1 tsp. salt season	seasons
½ cup molasses	1 tsp. garammasala
½ cup brown sugar	1 tsp. black pepper

Pick over bean to remove any foreign objects and soak Overnight in enough water to cove by 5 inches. Drain and Rinse the bean. In a large pot over medium heat, seasons The beans. Cook the beans 2 hour. Additional water to Cove. In a large skillet put the oil, onion. garlic, bell pepper Ground beef brown the meat, add the seasons tomato sauce. Pour the mixer in the large pot with the beans. Cook for 2 hour. Low heat.

Mashed Potatoes

2 potatoes[large]

1 cup cheese

1 tbsp. Garlic powder

1 tbsp. onion powder

1 tbsp. parsley[dry]

1 tbsp. butter

¼ cup cream

¼ cup ranch dressing

1 tsp. Salt

1 tsp. pepper

1 tsp. sugar

Peel the potatoes, cook the potatoes 30minutes. Mashed potatoes in a large bowl.combine all Ingredients in the bowl, serve

Mix Green

2 bunches collard green	4 cup water
2 bunches mustards green	2 tbsp. garlic
2 bunches turnips green	2 tbsp. onion
1 cup sugar	1 tbsp. thyme
½ cup vinegar	1 tsp. salt
2 tbsp. red pepper	2 tbsp. oil

Wash mix green thoroughly. Drain add water bring To boil with the mix green cove reduce heat add Remaining ingredients cook 30 minutes, or until all are tender. serve

Carolyn Jean Franklin Allen

Green Bean Casserole

1 cup green bean

2 cup potatoes[chopped]

1 cup bacon [chopped]

1 tbsp. bacon grease

½ cup onion

½ cup garlic

1 tsp. Nutmeg

1 tsp. brown sugar

½ tsp.black pepper

½ tsp. salt

In a skillet, cook the bacon, sauté garlic, onions Cook the potatoes, green bean until tender, add all Ingredients simmer over low heat 30minutes serve

Broccoli Casseroles

2 cup broccoli   1 cup cheese

2 cup rice   1 cup cream of broccoli

1 tsp. salt   1 tsp. black pepper

Cook the broccoli rice. Place the broccoli and rice In a large bowl add remaining ingredients. Place In a greased casserole bake for about 30minutes.

Squash & Banana

2 cup cheese

4 lb. squash

2 lb. banana

¼ cup sugar

3 eggs

½ cup bread crumbs

1 cup sour cream

¼ cup onion

½ cup butter

¼ cup garlic

½ tsp. pepper

½ tsp. salt

Cook the squash until tender into bake pan add The banana and squash all ingredient Preheat Oven 350 degree bake for 45 minutes.

Potatoes Cheese Casserole

4 cup potatoes[chopped]   1 tsp. salt

2 cup cheese   1 tsp. pepper

2 cup milk   1 tbsp. cornstarch

½ cup butter   ½ tbsp. chives

2 cup sour cream   ½ tbsp. garlic

Preheat to 350 degree spray the baking pan with cooking spray. Combine all wet ingredient into a large bowl and mix. Add the cornstarch to the mixture. Add all the ingredient into the mix. Pour the mixture into baking pan. Bake 40 minutes or until bubbly and golden brown.

Chicken Casserole

4 cup chicken[shredded]	1 cup nuts
2 cup carrots[shredded]	1 cup cream of chicken
2 cup squash[shredded]	1 tsp. poultry
1 cup cheese[shredded]	1 tsp. onion powder
1 bell pepper[chopped]	1 tsp. garlic powder
1 tsp. sage	1 tbsp. paprika
1/3 chicken broth	1 tbsp. parsley
1 tbsp. rosemary	1/3 tsp. salt & pepper

Cook the chicken in boiling ,salted water for 30 minutes, Remove the chicken out of the pot. Shredded chicken and put in a large bowl. Add All the seasons and other ingredients in the bowl Mix-well. Pour the chicken mixture into a greased Casserole dish. Bake at 350 degrees for 30 minutes.

Nikki-Poorman Casserole

2 cup rice

1 lb. beef[ground]

1 cup cheese [chopped]

1 tsp. cayenne pepper

1 jalapeno pepper

1 tsp. onion powder

1 tsp. chili powder

½ cup chili sauce

1 tbsp. cilantro

1 tsp. cumin

1 tbsp. parsley

1 tsp. garlic powder

In a large skillet put the oil and beef cook the meat for 15minutes.cook the rice for 10minutes.into a large bowl add the ingredients and mix. Serving,

Steak Casserole

1 lb. steak	2 tbsp. parsley
2 cup sweet potatoes	¼ tsp. sage
½ cup beef broth	1 tsp. Brown sugar
½ cup diced bacon	¼ tsp. nutmeg
1/3 cup bell pepper	¼ tsp. cumin
¼ cup onion	¼ tsp. salt & pepper
¼ cup garlic	¼ tsp. cardamom

Peel the sweet potatoes cut into slices. Put all the ingredients into a casserole with steak. And bake at 350 degree for 2 hour.

CJ'S Casserole

2 eggplant(medium)

2 cup pear(sliced)

1 lb. beer(ground)

1 cup oatmeal

½ cup tomatoes(diced)

½ cup beef broth

½ cup brown sugar

1/3 cup onion

1/3 cup garlic

½ cup walnut

1 tbsp. allspice

4 tbsp. butter

Brown the beef in a skillet, stirring occasionally. Into a large bowl, add all ingredients mix well, add the beef to the mixture. Pour the mixture into a baking dish. Bake at 325 degrees for 20 minutes.

Crawfish Casseroles

2 lb. crawfish	1 tsp. thyme
2 lb. crabmeat	1 tsp. chili powder
1 cup corn	¼ tsp. cayenne pepper
1 cup potatoes	¼ tsp. paprika
2 lb. shrimp	1 tbsp. lemon juice
2 tbsp. flour	1 tbsp. dry mustard
½ cup butter	1 tsp. Onion powder
¼ tsp. cloves(ground)	1 tsp. garlic powder

In a large pot add the crawfish, crabmeat, shrimp, bring to a boil let it cook for 10 minutes. Then turn off. Let the meat cool in the liquid. Into a bowl add all ingredient mix-well. Pour the mixture in a casserole bake at 350 degrees for 30 minutes.

Cracker And Cheese Casserole

5 lb. ground turkey

2 cup cracker crumbs

1 cup cheddar cheese

1 cup Monterey jack cheese

1 cup red bean

½ cup brown gravy

¼ cup bell pepper

¼ tsp. thyme

¼ cup onion

¼ cup garlic

3 tbsp. tomato paste

¼ tsp. cayenne pepper

2 tbsp. Pimentos

1 tbsp. Molasses

Brown the turkey and vegetables in a large skillet. Combine the ingredient into a bowl mix well. Pour the mixture in a casserole. Sprinkle with cracker and cheese on top. Bake at 350 degrees for 20 minutes.

Old-Time Family Casserole

1 lb. ground beef

1 lb. squash(sliced)

2 cup rice(cooked)

½ cup bacon(diced)

1 lb. black beans

1 cup tomatoes(diced)

½ lb. cheddar cheese

1 tsp. sage

1 tsp. curry powder

3 tbsp. soy sauce

¼ cup onion(diced)

¼ cup garlic(diced)

¼ cup bell pepper(diced)

½ tsp. basil

Cook veggie in 1 tbsp. hot fat until slightly browned. Add the ground beef and brown lightly. Mix all ingredients except cheese. Place in a casserole and top with cheese. Bake at 375 degree for 30 minutes.

Shanika Casseroles

4 cup shrimp

2 cup mango

1 cup avocado

1 cup tomatoes(diced)

1/3 cup heavy cream

1/3 cup butter

¼ cup minced onion

¼ cup minced garlic

1/3 cup celery(chopped)

1 tbsp. parley

¼ tsp. cayenne pepper

¼ tsp. Paprika

Cut the avocado into halves and remove seed. Peel and slice. Peel and slice mango. In a large bowl add shrimp and all ingredients mix-well. Pour the shrimp mixture into a greased casserole. Bake at 350 degrees for 30 minutes.

Rice Almond Casserole

2 cup rice

½ cup butter

1 cup almond

½ cup plain yogurt

3 eggs

2 tbsp. cardamom

½ tsp. Cinnamon

1 tsp. ginger

1 tsp. salt

½ cup sugar

Soak the rice for 20minute in warm water to cover Add 1tsp. Of the salt to remove some of the starch. Drain the rice. Add all the ingredient into the pot bring to a boil. Stir for 6 minutes until tender. Whisk the eggs into the mixture. Pour the mixture into a bake dish. Bake at 350 degrees for 20 minutes.

C.P.S. CASSEROLES

2 cup carrot

2 cup papaya

2 cup sweet potatoes

1 cup brown sugar

1 cup cheese

½ cup raisins

½ cup butter

¼ tsp. Mace

¼ tsp. nutmeg

¼ tsp. cinnamon

¼ tsp. Dry mustard

¼ tsp. ginger

¼ cup orange juice

1/3 cup almonds

Combine all ingredients and mix well. Pour into a greased casserole. Bake at 325 degrees for 1 hour.

Crab And Zucchini

2 cup zucchini

2 cup crabmeat

1/3 cup sour cream

1 cup cheese

2 tbsp. bread crumbs

2 tbsp. lemon juice

1 cup vegetable stock

½ cup artichoke

1 tsp. Creole mustard

1 tsp. Creole seasoning

¼ tsp. salt

¼ tsp. black pepper

2 tbsp. parsley

¼ cup vegetable oil

Into a large bowl slice 14-inch thick zucchini. Add the crabmeat and all the ingredients and mix. Pour the mixture into a casserole dish. Bake at 350 degrees for 40 minutes.

Seafood Casserole

1 cup shrimp

1 cup crabmeat

1 cup scallops

½ cup cream of shrimp

1/3 cup heavy cream

½ cup parmesan cheese

½ cup artichoke

1 tbsp. celery flaked

½ tsp. onion powder

½ tsp. garlic powder

¼ tsp. cayenne pepper

¼ tsp. lemon juice

½ cup dry bread crumbs

¼ cup pimento

Combine all the ingredients in a bowl and mix well. Pour into a grease casserole and top with bread crumbs and parmesan cheese. Bake at 350 degrees for 30 minutes.

Oyster Casserole

2 pt. oysters

2 cup cracker crumbs

½ cup butter

2/3 cup cream of shrimp

2 eggs

½ cup heavy cream

¼ tsp. celery flaked

¼ tsp. paprika

1 tbsp. parsley

1 tbsp. pimento

1 tsp. Worcestershire sauce

¼ tsp. old bay seasoning

Butter a casserole generously. Combine all the ingredients in a bowl and mixture into casserole. Bake at 350 degrees for 45 minutes.

Grits-Shrimp Casserole

2 cup grits

3 cup water

2 cup shrimp

½ cup butter

½ cup tomatoes(diced)

2 cup shredded cheese

¼ tsp. accent powder

1 tbsp. Old bay seasoning

1 cup heavy cream

½ cup cream of shrimp

¼ tsp. mace

3 eggs

Stir grits and salt into boiling water, cook until very thick. Cook the shrimp in boiling, water for 5 minutes, then drain. Beat eggs in mixing bowl. Add all the ingredient into the mixture. Pour into greased casserole. Top with remaining cheese. Bake at 350 degrees for 45 minutes.

Salmon & Mango Casserole

2 lb. salmon

2 cup mango(frozen)

¼ cup butter

1/3 cup cream

1 tsp. lemon juice

½ cup mango nectar

¼ cup onion

¼ cup garlic

¼ tsp. dill weed

1 tbsp. sugar

1 cup bread crumbs

1 tbsp. old bay seasoning

Grease the casserole in a large mix bowl combine all the ingredient and mix well. Pour the mixture into casserole dish. Bake at 350 degrees for 45 minutes.

Creole Casseroles

2 cup shrimps meat

2 cup crabs meat

2 cup sausages

1 cup black beans

1 cup red beans

1 cup com

1 cup okra

1 cup cream of celery

½ cup celery

1 tsp. cayenne pepper

1 tsp. Creole season

1 tsp. paprika

1 tsp. thyme

1 tsp. Parsley

1 tsp. Onion powder

1 tsp. Garlic powder

½ cup heavy cream

½ cup cream cheese

Cream all the wet ingredient. Combine all the ingredient together and mix. pour the mixture into baking pan bake 350 degrees for 30 minutes.

Asparagus Casserole

4 lb. asparagus

2 lb. shrimp

1 cup cream of shrimp

½ cup butter

½ cup heavy cream

1 cup grated cheese

¼ tsp. accent

¼ tsp. paprika

¼ tsp. cayenne pepper

1 tbsp. pimento

4 tbsp. cornstarch

¼ tsp. oregano

Cut up the asparagus in a bowl. Clean and boil the shrimp in water for 5 minutes. Drain and place in the bowl with the asparagus. Melt butter in a pot and stir in all remaining ingredients until smooth and thick. Pour the mixture into the bowl over the asparagus and shrimps and mix well. Pour the mixture in casserole and top with cheese. Bake at 400 degrees for 30 minutes.